David Arscott needs no introduction to anyone who knows Sussex. He lives in Lewes, and as a writer and broadcaster is well-known for the programmes he once produced and presented for BBC Radio Sussex. His books include more than two dozen on the history and wildlife of Sussex, he runs the highly successful Sussex Book Club and he publishes under his own Pomegranate Press imprint.

SUSSEX
BEDSIDE BOOK

*A Collection of Prose
and Poetry*

SELECTED AND INTRODUCED BY
DAVID ARSCOTT

THE DOVECOTE PRESS

First published in 2003 by The Dovecote Press Ltd
Stanbridge, Wimborne, Dorset BH21 4JD

ISBN 1 904349 22 6

Typeset in Monotype Sabon
Printed and bound by The Baskerville Press Ltd.
Salisbury, Wiltshire

A CIP catalogue record for this book is available
from the British Library

1 3 5 7 9 8 6 4 2

CONTENTS

INTRODUCTION

Some books involve more authorial toil than others, and this one (a confession to be made only after the publisher has put his signature to the contract) has been a breeze. An obvious reason is that most of the labour has already been undertaken by the writers whose works have been gratefully mined. Another is that any compiler of a Sussex anthology is spoilt for choice: has any county been more written about than ours? I had a first shot at the exercise some years ago with *In Praise of Sussex* (published by my own Pomegranate Press), and have found no difficulty whatsoever in avoiding significant repetitions here. The one glaring exception requires no apology – the *Sussex Bedside Book*, like its predecessor, has to begin with Rudyard Kipling's incomparable hymn to the history and topography of his adopted corner of England.

Starting out, I had only the vaguest idea of how the book would be organised, and which excerpts, sadly, would eventually have to be abandoned because they resisted comfortable submission to the thematic structure. The chosen themes are my own. I note that other titles in this Dovecote series have included chapters on war, crime and legends, topics which certainly appear in this volume, but fitfully and under other headings, while, for my part, I have grouped together writings on working life, sport and religion. Only as the project approached completion, however, did I realise that its predominant theme was a sense of place – landscape, towns, villages, roads, rivers, nature writing. Again, no apologies: much has changed in Sussex over the centuries, but its abiding physical beauties, natural and man-made, are paramount among what the native loves and the visitor is drawn to.

Although I hope this selection may lead you to some unfamiliar works (most available in public libraries and second-hand bookshops), my primary concern has been to provide pleasurable dip-in reading before you put out the light. For this reason the gentle and the celebratory unashamedly take precedent over the alarming and the grim, albeit not exclusively so. Sweet dreams . . .

DAVID ARSCOTT, *October* 2003

KIPLING'S 'SUSSEX'

God gave all men all earth to love,
    But, since our hearts are small,
Ordained for each one spot should prove
    Beloved over all;
That, as He watched Creation's birth,
    So we, in godlike mood,
May of our love create our earth
    And see that it is good.

So one shall Baltic pines content,
    As one some Surrey glade,
Or one the palm-grove's droned lament
    Before Levuka's Trade.
Each to his choice, and I rejoice
    The lot has fallen to me
In a fair ground – in a fair ground –
    Yea, Sussex by the sea!

No tender-hearted garden crowns,
    No bosomed woods adorn
Our blunt, bow-headed, whale-backed Downs,
    But gnarled and writhen thorn –
Bare slopes where chasing shadows skim,
    And through the gaps revealed,
Belt upon belt, the wooded, dim,
    Blue goodness of the Weald.

Clean of officious fence or hedge,
　　Half-wild and wholly tame,
The wise turf cloaks the white cliff-edge
　　As when the Romans came.
What sign of those that fought and died
　　At shift of sword and sword?
The barrow and the camp abide,
　　The sunlight and the sward.

Here leaps ashore the full Sou'west
　　All heavy-winged with brine,
Here lies above the folded crest
　　The channel's leaden line;
And here the sea-fogs lap and cling,
　　And here, each warning each,
The sheep-bells and the ship-bells ring
　　Along the hidden beach.

We have no waters to delight
　　Our broad and brookless vales –
Only the dewpond on the height
　　Unfed, that never fails –
Whereby no tattered herbage tells
　　Which way the season flies –
Only our close-bit thyme that smells
　　Like dawn in Paradise.

Here through the strong and shadeless days
　　The tinkling silence thrills;
Or little, lost, Down churches praise
　　The Lord who made the hills:
But here the Old Gods guard their round,
　　And in her secret heart,
The heathen kingdom Wilfrid found
　　Dreams, as she dwells, apart.

Though all the rest were all my share,
　　With equal soul I'd see
Her nine-and-thirty sister fair,
　　Yet none more fair than she.

Choose ye your need from Thames to Tweed,
  And I will choose instead
Such lands as lie 'twixt Rake and Rye,
  Black Down and Beachy Head.

I will go out against the sun
  Where the rollèd scarp retires,
And the Long Man of Wilmington
  Looks naked toward the shires;
And east till doubling Rother crawls
  To find the fickle tide,
By dry and sea-forgotten walls,
  Our ports of stranded pride.

I will go north about the shaws
  And the deep ghylls that breed
Huge oaks and old, the which we hold
  No more than Sussex weed;
Or south where windy Piddinghoe's
  Begilded dolphin veers,
And red beside wide-bankèd Ouse
  Lie down our Sussex steers.

So to the land our hearts we give
  Till the sure magic strike,
And Memory, Use, and Love make live
  Us and our field alike –
That deeper than our speech and thought,
  Beyond our reason's sway,
Clay of the pit whence we were wrought
  Yearns to its fellow-clay.

God gives all men all earth to love,
  But, since man's heart is small,
Ordains for each one spot shall prove
  Beloved over all.
Each to his choice, and I rejoice
  The lot has fallen to me
In a fair ground – in a fair ground –
  Yea, Sussex by the sea!

I · THE LANDSCAPE

The beauty of Sussex and the prodigious variety of its flora and fauna owe a great deal to the compexity of its surface soils – a wonderful jumble occasioned by a mighty upthrust of the landscape millions of years ago. It's a pleasure to give the first word on the subject to Esther Meynell, who has left us several fine books on a county she said was never a shire, 'but always a kingdom, complete in itself'.

The Geology of Sussex

The Downs are a rampart – beyond them the sea, behind them the Weald, the Hollow Land. In the remote geologic ages the whole outline and shape of this Sussex was different. The chalk Downs stretched, like an inverted bowl, across the whole county, from the South Downs to the North Downs. The Downs that we see now are but the rim, as it were, of that bowl, worn down by rain and wind and weather of all kinds, by the action of frost, the denudation of rivers – and by glaciers too, as some geologists hold – to the semblance we now know.

We are apt to think, owing to the inadequacy and limited outlook of the majority of the history books on which we were brought up, that the history of a country – and the history of a county is but the same thing on a smaller scale – is caused and created by the men who inhabited it, by its kings and heroes. That is a most lopsided idea, as a certain number of people are beginning to perceive. Geology, except to its devoted students, has a somewhat dull and difficult air, with a memory of the lifeless aspect of 'specimens' in glass cases, all neatly labelled and conveying little to the uninstructed eye. But geology is really the foundation of everything – 'Dust we are, and unto dust we return'. Out of that dust, out of the Chalk and the Greensand and the Gault Clay was Sussex formed. Because of these geological formations Sussex scenery – so varied and so different in different parts of the county – was created by time and weather, and upheavals of the earth's crust, and sinkings under the sea. There the men who were to be Sussex men, little as they knew it in their dim and dawning days, discovered that they could live a precarious existence in certain parts of Sussex and not in others: that water was to be found in certain places and not in others; that the springs 'broke' at certain times – though they knew nothing of a 'watertable' – that dry stream-beds became 'winterbournes'.

Esther Meynell; Sussex (1947)

Duncton Hill

Hilaire Belloc, like so many of our best-loved Sussex authors, was an incomer, or 'furriner'. The son of a French father and an English mother, he spent his boyhood at Slindon and, as an adult, brought his family first to Slindon and then to Shipley, where he died in 1953. This poem concludes his idiosyncratic book The Four Men, *which relates a fictitious walk from the George Inn at Robertsbridge west to the Hampshire border, and bustles with humour, argument and song.*

He does not die that can bequeath
Some influence to the land he knows,
Or dares, persistent, interwreath
Love permanent with the wild hedgerows;
    He does not die, but still remains
    Substantiate with his darling plains.

The spring's superb adventure calls
His dust athwart the woods to flame;

His boundary river's secret falls
Perpetuate and repeat his name.
> He rides his loud October sky:
> He does not die. He does not die.

The beeches know the accustomed head
Which loved them, and a peopled air
Beneath their benediction spread
Comforts the silence everywhere;
> For native ghosts return and these
> Perfect the mystery in the trees.

So, therefore, though myself be crosst
The shuddering of that dreadful day
When friend and fire and home are lost
And even children drawn away –
> The passer-by shall hear me still
> A boy that sings on Duncton Hill.

Hilaire Belloc; The Four Men (1912)

Walking on the Downs

The journalist and broadcaster S.P.B. Mais spent the second half of his life in Southwick. A keen walker, he wrote lively books in praise of the open-air life. Here he describes the villages at the foot of the Downs.

The South Downs unfold their beauties and reveal their mysteries only to the walkers – men of the stamp of Mr Charles Vince, who in *Wayfarers in Arcady* entices us once more to leave the beaten highway and explore that mysterious, aloof, long, unwavering line that cuts off the sea from the weald . . .

The very names of the villages at their feet have a Shakespearean ring about them: 'Midhurst and Petworth, Amberley, Bramber, Wilmington, Friston, Beddingham and Glynde. What more do you want to know of any place than its name and how far it is to go there?'

Yet how thankful we are when we are on the heights to feel that men will never go up a hill when they can go down. The shepherds are the only living souls we meet, and they, we feel, are the only men who could be in tune with our moods, for we are transfigured as soon as we tread the soft, clean-clipped green turf, and a benign calm descends on our souls.

The villages in the valley may have haunting names, but we have no wish to go down to them. Ecstasy is ours as the warm west wind blows through our hair, as some fresh, unforgettable vision swims into our ken, the vague outline of the Isle of Wight from Chanctonbury, the setting sun on Chichester Cathedral seen through a gap from Rackham Hill, the stern grandeur of Arundel Castle rising from the trees, the sweet suddenness of Telscombe, Mr Vince's 'village at the world's end', as you fall into it over the brim of Highdole Hill, the quiet splendour of Friston Place and Highden House and Parham.

If you want to fall head over ears in love with the country that is your own, walk out of your house or hotel in Eastbourne or Brighton, step out of the train at Amberley or Lewes, go to Findon, Storrington or Steyning and just climb the nearest hill. In half-an-hour all the pack of burdens that weighs you down in the valley will have fallen from your shoulders. You are now made free of the earth and the sky and the sea. All human worries will seem petty trifles. Wander at your will, forget direction and time. When your eye is diverted from the track, follow it; lie down and listen to the larks, the gulls, the wash of the sea on the pebbles below the cliff edge, and the sheep bells. Let your eyes feast on the riot of colours from the poppies and the mustard, on the rounded curves, so bare and austere in their beauty, of the rolling Downs.

S.P.B. Mais; 'The Sussex Downs' from Oh, to be in England (1922)

The Downsman

Arthur Beckett was a journalist, author and newspaper proprietor (the Eastbourne Gazette *and other papers), a founder member of the Society of Sussex Downsmen and for many years editor of that storehouse of county lore, the* Sussex County Magazine.

The Downsman climbs the bostal and reaches the rim of the hill,
He is lord of the land, of the Sussex land, from Beachy to Selsey Bill,

He has gotten these hills from his forebears, who won them by dint
of sword,
And dear to him is the Wealden plain, and dear is the Downland
sward.

Great is the gift, his forebears' gift; the Downsman swells with
pride
As he looks on the land, the Sussex land, stretched far from the
steep hill-side;
He owns not a sod, not a single sod, from hence to the sounding
shore,
Yet he's lord of the land, of the fair, wide land once drenched with
his fathers' gore.

From Duncton Down to Tarberry Hill the Downs are white with
sheep,
Red kine lie in the marshlands, and stand in the grassways deep;
He owns not a beast, not a single beast, and yet he is lord of all,
His forebears were of the shepherd race of Sussex pastoral.

The Downsman looks on the plain below, where 'mong a thousand
trees
A hundred grey-green villages lie dozing 'pon the lease;
He has but one roof, a humble roof, no more than a simple cot,
But his forebears built the villages, and he's lord of them all, God
wot.

Arthur Beckett; 'The Downsman' from The Spirit of the Downs *(1909)*

The Mythology of Downland

*Here's a gentle corrective to the above by a landscape historian – but
mercifully one who loves the Downs and lives within sight of them.*

The South Downs are no ordinary hills. They are perhaps the most
familiar hills in England and before the mid-1920s they were regarded
as its most beautiful stretch of downland. Their exquisitely smooth yet
deeply sculpted landscape imbued with the tang of the sea remained
unspoiled, its loveliness only enhanced by man-made associations

arising from its bountiful corn and Southdown sheep. Although prized as the jewel of the Sussex crown, eulogising by Rudyard Kipling, Hilaire Belloc and many others ensured that they were not merely of local but of national, even international importance. With 19th-century urbanisation the rhythmically-rolling Downs came to be regarded as peculiarly and beguilingly English, the landscape of dreams. Consequently, few landscapes have spoken so potently to each generation to transpose their inspirational and spiritual qualities into verse, landscape painting or orchestral sounds. To Arthur Mee, the far-travelled editor of the King's England series of inter-war county books, Sussex was 'the county of counties for sheer English beauty' and the South Downs 'the natural glory of our island'. So many similar public declarations were made that Hilaire Belloc claimed the South Downs as a national institution which lifted people's experience of them to something approaching a religious creed. Drenched in verse, 'country writing', painting, photography and advertising, and promoted with no hyperbole too great, Kipling's 'blunt, bow-headed, whale backed downs' were created into a national icon of a landscape regarded as quintessentially English, which men and women from all over the Empire thought about when they were most homesick and where they planned to end their lives. In the English arts and crafts world the Downs had a special resonance and they became a major part of a national identity for an urban society with a taste for Old England, nostalgically harking back to a past rural idyll. For these various reasaons the downs became world-renowned as a focus of English culture.

The images that sustained this nostalgic idea of the South Downs so healingly to the heart were a kind of golden dream based on a half-imagined, half-recollected, notion of pastoral England. In this dream the real and the tangible merged with the imagined to such a degree that the Downs became as much a state of mind, like Atlantis, Utopia or Brigadoon, as a physical reality. Thus the history of the Downs is full of myths.

Peter Brandon; The South Downs *(1998)*

Sketching on the Downs

G.K. Chesterton, drawing on sheets of brown paper, discovers that his collection of chalks lacks the vital colour, white.

I sat on the hill in a sort of despair. There was no town nearer than Chichester at which it was even remotely probable that there would be such a thing as an artist's colour-man. And yet, without white, my absurd little pictures would be as pointless as the world would be if there were no good people in it. I stared stupidly round, racking my brain for expedients. Then I suddenly stood up and roared with laughter, again and again, so that the cows stared at me and called a committee. Imagine a man in the Sahara regretting that he had no sand for his hour-glass. Imagine a gentleman in mid-ocean wishing that he had brought some salt water with him for his chemical experiments. I was sitting on an immense warehouse of white chalk. The landscape was made entirely out of white chalk. White chalk was piled mere miles until it met the sky. I stopped and broke a piece off the rock I sat on; it did not mark so well as the shop chalks do; but it gave the effect. And I stood there in a trance of pleasure, realising that this Southern England is not only a grand peninsula, and a tradition and a civilisation; it is something even more admirable. It is a piece of chalk.

G.K. Chesterton; Tremendous Trifles

The Wind on the Downs

Tickner Edwardes walked out on his father's import/export business to live in a cottage at Burpham, near Arundel, where he wrote closely observed books and articles on country life. He later entered the priesthood, becoming vicar of Burpham in 1927.

To get the true spirit of the Sussex Downs, you must become a lover of the wind, loving it in all its moods. There are rare moments, even on Windle Hill, when the sun glows in a halcyon sky, and the blue air about you lies as still and silent as a sheltered woodland mere. But this is not true Downland weather. A calm day in the valleys may stand for tranquillity, and be well enough; but here it savours rather of stagnation. The very life of the Downs is in their flowing, ever-changing atmosphere – the sweet pure current coming to you unwinnowed over a visible course of twenty miles. When the wind is still, it is good to keep to the lowlands, under their green canopies of whispering leaves, within sound of their purling undertone of brooks; for the valley has its own companionable voices of earth, even under silent skies. But the Downs are as a strung harp, that will yield no music save to the touch of one gargantuan player. Their very essence of life is in the careering air. You must learn to love the wind for its own sake, or you will never come to be a true Sussex highlander – to know what the magic is that brings Sussex men, meeting by chance in some far-off nook of the world, to talk first of all of the Downs, when, in the stifling heat of a tropic night, or by northern camp-fires, pipes are aglow, and tired hearts wistfully homing.

Tickner Edwardes; Neighbourhood *(1911)*

The South Down Sheep

It seems fitting to include at least one piece about sheep in this chapter, because their vast flocks were once so characteristic of the downland landscape. Rev Arthur Young was a leading agricultural reformer who later became First Secretary to the Board of Agriculture, although he managed to ruin his own East Anglian farm through a series of experiments. The South Down breed was perfected by John Ellman of Glynde.

The South Down farmers breed their sheep with faces and legs of a colour just as suits their fancy. One likes black, another sandy, a third speckled, and one and all exclaim against white. This man concludes that legs and faces with an inclination to white are infallible signs of tenderness, and do not stand against the severity of the weather with the same hardiness as the darker breed; and they allege that these sorts will fall off in their flesh. A second will set the first right, and pronounce that in a lot of weathers those that are soonest and most fat are white faced; that they prove remarkable good milkers; but that white is an indication of a tender breed. Another is of the opinion that, by breeding the lambs too black, the wool is injured, and likewise apt to be tainted with black, and spotted, especially about the neck, and not saleable. A fourth breeds with legs and faces as black as it is possible; and he too is convinced that the healthiness is in proportion to blackness; whilst another says that if the South Downs sheep were suffered to run in a wild state they would in a very few years become absolutely black. All these are opinions of eminent breeders: in order to reconcile them, others breed for speckled faces; and it is the prevailing colour.

It is merely mentioned with a view of pointing out the various opinions which prevail. The stupidity of shepherds we do not wonder at; but that they should be able to impose these prejudices on their masters, is more surprising.

Let it be observed that in the flocks in Sussex grey, speckled, or mottled faces and legs, generally prevail, but any sheep with white faces or legs, though in other respects an unexceptionable animal, would not be esteemed.

Arthur Young; General View of the Agriculture of the County of Sussex (1813)

The Colonisation of the Weald

Such is the reputation of the Downs that the Weald is often relegated to second place in people's affections. Yet it's a richly varied area, crossed by rivers and encompassing high ridges, deep valleys and heavily wooded flatlands. As a boy Ben Darby traversed it time and again on his bicycle.

The Romans knew the Weald as a wild and hostile place and they called it Silva Anderida. They drove one main highway across it which the Saxons later named Stane Street (Stone Street). They built a number of secondary roads, probably for carrying out iron from mines worked by the Celts. They also built posting stations, but in all the wild region they established no main centre. it was the tough, rough and unsophisticated Saxons, with their hefty if clumsy implements, who began the systematic settlement and cultivation of the great wild, which they called Andredsweald. The Venerable Bede (AD 673–735) called the forest Andred's Weald, and 'Andred' had probably been taken over from the Celts. There may be an association with the Roman 'Anderida', but it would be unwise to assume this. The Anglo-Saxon Chronicle estimates the extent of 'the great wood which we call Andred' at about 120 miles east to west and about thirty broad.

Big roads from London cut through the Weald on their way to the coast, alien things, belonging to no countryside. Yet even on these fast highways you see enough to realise that you are passing through a land of very great interest though speed denies you the time to appreciate its beauty. If, however, you strike off the main roads, east or west, in an astonishingly short distance you find yourself travelling along small winding lanes, and on many of these two cars can pass only with great difficulty. Before the war a good half of these lanes were not made up and some still are not. Depending on which part of the county you are in, they may take you over heathland, through forest with the trees meeting overhead, or between meadows and small arable fields. They link together villages and hamlets, and it is possible to motor through the length of Sussex, east to west, and scarcely touch a main road except to cross it. On such a journey, of course, haste must be discounted.

All the villages and hamlets in the Weald, except those on the major roads, have one thing in common: they seem to have grown there, like the trees. This is not just a flight of fancy; it contains an element of truth. Through the centuries, villages and nature in the Weald have fused, each depending on the other and both together building up a particular kind of countryside. First, the clearing in the forest, the modest homestead and the huts, both of the timber ready to hand; presently the church, a bigger homestead, a bigger clearing, and huts replaced by substantial cottages. Farms gradually grew larger, cottages more numerous; the forest slowly thinned, drainage dried the bogs.

Ben Darby; View of Sussex (1975)

The Unchanging Weald

The nature of the soil, absence of good communications and tardy exploitation of minerals are reflected in the character of the cultivated landscape as we see it today. Had it been practicable in early times to construct a really good direct highway from Horsham to the old ports of Rye and Winchelsea, the development of Mid-Sussex might have been accelerated. As it is, the long hard-won struggle to cultivate the Wealden belt has taken nearly five hundred years to accomplish. A complex network of tortuous roads improved from the old pioneer tracks still represents the only means of communication between many village settlements which owe their origin to forest clearings or the presence of iron-stone. The advent of the railways to the coast in the last century introduced gradually that suburban element of population which had previously invaded Surrey, and both Burgess Hill and Haywards Heath belong to this period; their population looks mainly to London for a livelihood rather than to the soil of the Weald. For the most part the Wealden villages are still agriculture communities; and the farms have changed but little since the eighteenth century. Arable fields have here and there given place to pasture as in other counties, but the field boundaries with their 'shaws' or protecting borders of woodland remain much as they have been since first carved out of the medieval forests.

The Weald is no place for the motorist in search of speedways. On the other hand, there is a wealth of material to be found by those with leisure on a long summer's day, either on foot or by car. It is a countryside of well-watered meadows and pastures, short, sturdy oaks or tall elms, little streams which slowly meander through bird-haunted, reedy margins until reluctantly they pay tribute to Arun, Adur or Ouse; and among these tributaries we commend the loveliest of Sussex streams – the Western Rother, which, although born among the uplands of Hampshire, enriches the countryside from Rogate to the Arun at Pulborough. All the little wealden villages lie close to one or other of the many streams, although their builders, with an eye to a well-drained site, avoided any land that might suffer ccasional floods. Chithurst, Trotton with its splendid bridge, Iping, Stedham and Woolbeding all stand well above the winter floods, and they have the benefit of sandy soil rather than the heavy clay, as at Kirdford, Loxwood and Wisborough.

W. Harding Thompson & Geoffrey Clark; The Sussex Landscape *(1935)*

Chanclebury Ring

Wilfrid Scawen Blunt was a man of the West Sussex Weald, born at Crabbet Park in 1840. He had the last few lines of this poem (the title is dialect for Chanctonbury Ring) inscribed on his tomb at Newbuildings Place, Southwater. A friend of Belloc, he was an amateur diplomat, horse-breeder and Arabist as well as a poet.

> Say what you will, there is not in the world
> A nobler sight than from his upper down.
> No rugged landscape here, no beauty hurled
> From its Creator's hand as with a frown;
> But a green plain on which green hills look down
> Trim as a garden plot. No other hue
> Can hence be seen, save here and there the brown
> Of a square fallow, and the horizon's blue.
> Dear checker-work of woods, the Sussex Weald.
> If a name thrills me yet of things on earth,
> That name is thine! How often I have fled
> To thy deep hedgerows and embraced each field,
> Each lag, each pasture – fields which gave me birth
> And saw my youth, and which must hold me dead.

Wilfrid Scawen Blunt; 'Chanclebury Ring'

Ashdown Forest

The Weald of Sussex has been called 'the place where London ends and England can begin,' and there is no question that Ashdown Forest, an integral part of the Weald, forms the finest stretch of open heathland within seventy miles of the capital. Here it is still possible to enjoy solitude without queueing for it, to walk or ride for half a day and seldom meet another person, to drive along roads bordering private woodland where 200 fallow deer dwell, and to explore on foot ten square miles of dry, damp and wet heathland – 6,400 acres – harbouring distinctive plant and animal communities that are an endless source of wonder and delight to the keen observer, whether he is a professional scientist, an amateur naturalist or a casual walker.

For the increasing hosts of visitors who picnic on the edge of the heath, the almost bare, windswept slopes of the forest offer splendid views far across the well-wooded Weald to the South Downs which, from this distance, almost justify Gilbert White's description of them as a 'vaste range of mountains'. In late summer colonies of bog asphodel infuse the sphagnum bogs with a golden glow and wisps of white cotton grass bend before the winds. The rare marsh gentians flourish on a few stretches of damp heath, though their numbers tend to fluctuate for reasons not yet explained. On warm summer nights when moths are abundant, the weird churring and wing-clapping of nightjars may be heard amid the bracken and gorse. Occasionally the odd pair of hobbies nesting in some scattered clump of Scots pines may be seen pouncing upon the grasshoppers and dragonflies; and the evocative calls of nesting curlews are sometimes heard amid the bleached purple moorgrass and heather where blackcock bred until a century ago.

Ashdown Forest, however, can never be fully appreciated if it is regarded only as a pleasant landscape that is the source of spiritual and physical renewal for visitors from the towns. It also forms the home of a population that includes more than a thousand Commoners, though fewer than fifty of them now exercise their ancient rights to cut bracken, heather and grass, to graze cattle and pigs, or to claim birch, willow and alder for fuel and repair on their own holdings.

Garth Christian; Ashdown Forest *(1967)*

On the Marshes

At its western end Sussex has the flat Chichester plain, bordering a large harbour with several natural inlets. At the eastern end is more low-lying land, the Walland Marsh around Rye forming part of Romney Marsh, which spreads into Kent.

Romney Marsh is one of the three great coastal marshlands of southern England. In common with the Fens of East Anglia and the Somerset Levels, and also the Humber lowlands, the marshlands of north-west England and numerous other smaller areas round our coasts, almost all of this large area lies below the level of high tides and has always been under threat of flooding by the sea or fresh water; [William] Dugdale's picturesque 'deluge of waters'. But in one respect Romney Marsh is exceptional, and differs from the other major marshlands. It alone developed and was originally occupied in the shelter behind wide barriers of flint pebbles, known as shingle. These barriers provided not only essential protection for the low-lying land, but also shelter for once-large anchorages on which ports were based. However, rounded pebbles are moved all too easily by the waves and therefore on a large scale the barriers themselves moved. Thus a feature which had provided essential protection in one century often became a liability in the next.

So where and what is Romney Marsh? It forms the south-east corner of England, and in the widest sense includes 100 square miles (27,000ha) stretching 20 miles (32km) from the cliffs near Fairlight in the south-west to those at Hythe in the north-east. On the south and east it is bounded by the English Channel, with the great shingle promontory of Dungeness jutting out towards France. On the west and north is an old cliff line cut into the Wealden upland. Additional fingers of marshland extend up to 10 miles (16km) westward along the valleys of three rivers, the Rother, Tillingham and Brede, with the rivers providing important arteries into and out of the hinterland. This great expanse is subdivided into several smaller area, whose names generally date from the different times at which they were reclaimed from the sea or when an autonomous authority was established to manage their drainage.

Jill Eddison; Romney Marsh, Survival on a Frontier *(2001)*

2 · SUSSEX BY THE SEA

It's a bright and breezy phrase, but the sea has been the neighbour from hell as often as it has been the bringer of gifts. Here we explore its manifold influences on the county and its people. George Aitchison, who starts us off with a robust and somewhat fanciful piece (can we really detect that Celtic breed?), edited the Sussex Express.

The All-powerful Sea

The sea was the creator of Sussex. The sea is ever the destroyer of Sussex. Time was when man could walk dry-footed, not only from Calais to Dover, but from Brighton to Boulogne. The rollers from the Atlantic bored their way up the English Channel. The waves of the North Sea bit out the straits of Dover. At last the two seas met, and England was an island. . . . The last land-bridge or isthmus that joined England to France was made of the Wealden Rocks of Hastings.

It was the sea that peopled Sussex with the folk to be found within its borders today. By the sea from Belgium came those folk of the Iron Age, men of Celtic breed, dark and ductile as their iron. You may detect traces of them today, so some of us hold, wherever along the coast a short dark people, with some liveliness of manner and thought, are to be found mixed with the dominant flaxen-haired Saxons, of gently bovine minds and singing speech. Celtic words are embedded like curious fossils in the prevalent chalk of the Saxon speech. Adur and Arun, Combe and Glynde, came long before the 'ings' and the 'hams' and the 'worths'.

It was the sea that brough the Romans, to colonise and cultivate, to make Sussex, with other parts of England, a willing and working partner in their great Empire. Are there any clearer signs of the reality of the Roman occupation of Britain, for a period longer than between Queen Elizabeth and Queen Victoria, than its intense cultivation of the fertile belt of land between the Downs and the sea?

From the humble farmstead of Roman times at Brighton to the palatial villa at Bignor, there ran a continuous chain of settlements, where the Roman civilisation worked side by side with Celtic labour in an intense, highly commercialised farming.

Much of this farm produce was for export by sea-borne traffic. In those days, probably more than in any other, Sussex was conscious of her place by the sea and her union with the coast on the other side of that sea, while roadless forest and marsh separated her from the rest of the island.

The sea brought the Saxon, Aella and Cissa and Wlencing and the whole fierce flaxen brood that followed, until by raid after raid, battle after battle, fury after fury, even the shadow of the Celtic name flickered and faded out before that destroying blaze, and the land became wholly and solely the Saxon land – the South Saex, the Sussex of all the following centuries. The sea brought the Dane, who has left more vestiges in Sussex than is often realised.

It was at Hastings that the sea won its final battle over the resisting land and made England an island – geographically independent of France and the rest of the continent of Europe. It was at Hastings that William the Bastard, brought by the sea, landed, gained a single and final victory over the Saxons and made England politically dependent on France and united to the rest of the mainland of the Continent.

Yet the sea that made Sussex is also the sea that is destroying Sussex. The sea gave, the sea has taken away. The history of the coast of Sussex, from Chichester Harbour to Beachy Head, is the history of continuous destruction by the sea. The waves that cut through the Straits of Dover have striven ever to widen the gap. It is no exaggeration to say that, since Julius Caesar made his first landing on the southern shores of Britain, the coast of Sussex has been driven back by the sea for at least one mile . . . All the way along the coast, as one sails eastwards, a coasting vessel will pass over the sites of vanished hamlets.

The history of Brighton, as far back as it is recorded, is a history of vanished acres. There cannot be any doubt that the original Saxon settlement of Brighthelm is now under the sea. What must have been the 'Bungalow Town' of those days – shacks built on the shingle – was completely swept away by the storm of 1703. The coastal road at Black Rock, to the east of Brighton, was, within living memory, divided from the sea by enough land for a cricket field, with the pitch running north and south. . . Thanks, however, to the energies of county councils, borough councils and their engineers, the more physical attack of the sea may now be counted as at an end.

But if the sea has been beaten physically, it is still, in more subtle fashion, destroying the Sussex coast. The lure of the Sussex sea has brought not only the day tripper, but the tripper-turned-resident, who builds himself a shack or converts a railway carriage, and performs other unsightly tricks that turn the beauty of the coast into a desolation and a shame. That same lure has brought the building speculator, the estate developer, some with high intelligence, some in the densest ignorance. The baffled sea in revenge has brought the town.

George Aitchison; Sussex (1936)

Fashionable Hastings

The poet Thomas Hood and his wife, Jane, spent their honeymoon in Hastings in 1825, and he later wrote 30 eight-line stanzas about the up-and-coming resort. The culmination of his poem is a violent storm, but here is the opening, with its picture of 'the fashion' in their pomp.

'Twas August – Hastings every day was filling –
Hastings that 'greenest spot on memory's waste!'
With crowds of idlers willing or unwilling
To be bedipped – be noticed – or be braced.
And all things rose a penny in a shilling.
Meanwhile, from window and from door, in haste

'Accommodation bills' kept coming down,
Gladding 'the world of letters' in that town.

Each day pour'd in new coach-fulls of new cits.
Flying from London smoke and dust annoying.
Unmarried Misses hoping to make hits,
And new-wed couples fresh from Tunbridge toying.
Lacemen and placemen, ministers and wits,
And quakers of both sexes, much enjoying
A morning's reading by the ocean's rim,
That sect delighting in the sea's broad brim.

Thomas Hood; 'A Storm at Hastings'

Middleton

Charlotte Smith (1749–1806) had heroic qualities which were put to the test throughout her life. Had she been a man she would doubtless have made much more of an artistic mark (although, as it was, Wordsworth praised her poetry) but at the age of 15 she was married to the feckless Benjamin Smith, and for the rest of the days she had to cope with his inadequacies while raising a large family on little money. Regarding herself as 'a pearl that had been basely thrown away,' she wrote determinedly with financial security in mind, producing 32 volumes of novels and a number of children's books within the space of eight years. These lines were written after a visit to the practically deserted coastal village of Middleton in West Sussex.

The wild blast rising from the western cave
Drives the huge billows from their heaving bed,
Tears from their grassy tomb the village dead,
And breaks the silent sabbath of the grave!
With shells and sea-weed mingled on the shore,
Lo, their bones whiten in the frequent wave;
But vain to them the wind and waters rave,
They hear the warring elements no more.

Charlotte Smith

Washed Away

Gerard Young was a regular visitor to Sussex before he bought a run-down cottage at Flansham, near Bognor, and made it habitable. He wrote a book about his experiences, and several more followed, while his regular employment was as a journalist with the Bognor Post.

Men have been altering the aspect of the Sussex coast within comparatively recent times, but the sea has been taking its toll for centuries. The slow drag and undertow of the waves have a strength against which breakwaters seem still to be a puny safeguard. There are few things more amazing than the vanishing of shingle beaches overnight. I used to notice this at Worthing when I was a boy. The force of the waves alone as they crashed onto the beach near the bandstand used to awe me and I can still sense that eerie tug of the receding turf around my ankles.

We had our favourite spots among the pebbly slopes and valleys of the beach, often in the lee of a breakwater. I might note a site for future occupation and return next day to find the pebble contours competely changed. Great new banks of brown and white stones had arrived from somewhere, or else the space of the breakwater had been swept almost clear of shingle and we had smooth sand in return. Thousands of tons disappear each day from Sussex beaches and are deposited elsewhere. It is one form of perpetual motion and thus the Hampshire shingle feeds the shoreline of Sussex and the Sussex pebbles in turn are swept along eastwards to build up Dungeness.

Not only the shingle goes, but also the land. There is much of Sussex under the sea. Unceasingly the tides devour the shingle mounds, the banks of drifted sand and the beds of clay that form the miniature cliffs of the sea plain. Look westwards from this hill again at Selsey Bill. Today you can see its grey-green broad shape curving out into the shallow sea, with the flash of sun on the creeks of Chichester Harbour beyond. The Selsey on which the Saxons landed was much further southward than it is now. The submerged Owers Bank, beyond which now rides a lightship, is identifiable with Cymenes ora, the place where Ella first put foot in Sussex.

Gerard Young; 'On Nore Hill in Summertime', from The Cottage in the Fields *(1946)*

Old Winchelsea

Severe storms in the middle of the thirteen century led to the abandonment of the old port of Winchelsea which stood on the levels somewhere in the region of present day Camber Sands. It must have been situated on a bend in the River Brede, as the place-name comes from the Old English 'wincel', or 'corner', and 'eye', which means island.

The earliest recorded storms – in October 1250 – brought high tides that submerged part of the town, whilst the second and more devastating storm of October 1287 caused the River Rother to divert its course. Until that time it had flowed north of the Isle of Oxney to an estuary at New Romney in Kent, but the storm threw up a shingle bank there, and the river found a new course south of Oxney to meet the sea at Winchelsea, washing most of it away in the process.

Edward I had already started to lay out a replacement town. In 1280 he had acquired the manor of Iham on a hilltop position three miles to the north-west. In September 1292 the burgage plots were finally handed over by the Bishop of Ley, acting on behalf of the King, who in turn gave them a helping hand in the establishment of a new town by allowing its residents the first seven years rent free. Much has been written about the new Winchelsea, and it seems likely that it was never fully occupied, and that the King went back on his promise by charging full rents almost from the start.

The town was planned on a large scale, with over 40 houses in the north-east corner having vaulted cellars to house barrels of wine imported from Gascony – the trade on which the new town was to depend for its prosperity. There were orginally three churches, the largest of which – and only survivor – St Thomas's, was allotted a whole block on the street grid.

After such a well-planned start the later history of Winchelsea is one of steady decline. The River Brede, which linked the town to the coast, started to silt up, creating very difficult harbour access. To compound their problems the townsfolk suffered four raid by the French, during which a large part of St Thomas's Church was destroyed. By the sixteenth century there were less than 60 inhabited houses, and today less than a third of the original burgage plots may be seen.

John Vigar; The Lost Villages of Sussex (1994)

Fashionable Brighton

Brighton was the greatest of the seaside resorts in the early 19th century – and many would make the same claim for it today. The sea-water cure and royal patronage encouraged wealthy visitors to flock to the coast in droves, where many would be plunged under the waves by an army of 'dippers', the most famous of whom are remembered in this anonymous doggerel.

> There's plenty of dippers and jockers
> And salt water rigs for your fun,
> The king of them all is Old Smoaker,
> The queen of them all Martha Gunn.
> The ladies walk out in the morn
> To taste of the salt water breeze,
> They ask if the water is warm ,
> Says Martha: 'Yes, ma'am, if you please'.
> Then away to the machines they run
> 'Tis surprising how soon they get stript.
> I oft wish myself Martha Gunn
> Just to see the young ladies get dipt.

Everybody who is anybody goes to Brighton. It is the pet seaside resort of aristocratic and democratic Londoners, only the latter visit it chiefly in the summer time, the former when 'town is empty', and the bracing wind of December blows freshly and keenly over the Sussex Downs . . . There is a favourite *locale* – where Brill's well-known baths jut out into awkward prominency, and the seawall takes a sudden sweep. There the waters surge up in stormy grandeur, rising defiantly against the barrier opposed by the industry of man, and flinging their glittering spray with savage deight over the pedestrians and equestrians who attempt this difficult 'pass'.

How the wind does sweep and howl! How it tantalises the crinoline-encompassed belles, and cavaliers who – between mad efforts to keep their hats upon their heads, and to manage their steeds with the requisite grace – are driven to the extremes of desperation! On a stormy day, when the wind is up Channel, do not attempt to pass Brill's baths unless you have an easy seat and a firm hand! We have seen equestrian neophytes, at this particular point, reduced to sudden ignominy and irremediable disgrace when most exultant.

Illustrated London News; *January 1st 1859*

Sanditon

Jane Austen set her unfinished novel Sanditon *somewhere between Eastbourne and Hastings, although it has been reasonably suggested that she had in mind the experience of the unfortunate Sir Richard Hotham at Bognor* (see page 135). *Her ear is characteristically sharp.*

'My name is Parker – Mr Parker of Sanditon; this lady, my wife, Mrs Parker. We are on our road home from London. *My* name perhaps, tho' I am by no means the first of my family, holding landed property in the parish of Sanditon, may be unknown at this distance from the coast, but Sanditon itself – everybody has heard of Sanditon – the favourite for a young and rising bathing-place, certainly the favourite spot of all that are to be found along the coast of Sussex – the most favoured by Nature, and promising to be the most chosen by Man.'

'Yes, I have heard of Sanditon,' replied Mr H. 'Every five years, one hears of some new place or other starting up by the sea, and growing the fashion. How they can half of them be filled is the wonder! *Where* people can be found with money or time to go to them! Bad things for a country – sure to raise the price of provisions and make the poor good for nothing, as I dare say you find, sir.'

'Not at all Sir, not at all,' cried Mr Parker eagerly. 'Quite the contrary I assure you. A common idea, but a mistaken one. It may apply to your large, overgrown places like Brighton, or Worthing or East Bourne, but *not* to a small village like Sanditon, precluded by its size from experiencing any of the evils of civilization, while the growth of the place, the buildings, the nursery grounds, the demand for every thing, and the sure resort of the very best company, those regular, steady, private families of thorough gentility and character, who are a blessing everywhere, excite the industry of the poor, and diffuse comfort and improvement among them of every sort. No sir, assure you, Sanditon is not a place –'

'I do not mean to take exceptions to *any* place in particular, sir,' answered Mr H. 'I only think our coast is too full of them altogether. But had we not better try to get you –'

'Our coast too full!' repeated Mr P. 'On that point perhaps we may not totally disagree; at least there are *enough*. Our coast is abundant enough; it demands no more. Everybody's taste and everybody's finances may be suited. And those good people who are trying to add to the number are, in my opinion, excessively absurd, and must soon find themselves the dupes of their own fallacious calculations. Such a place as Sanditon, sir, I may say, was wanted, was called for. Nature had marked it out – had spoken in most intelligible characters. The finest, purest sea breeze on the coast – acknowledged to be so – excellent bathing – fine hard sand – deep water ten yards from the shore – no mud – no weeds – no slimy rocks. Never was there a place more palpably designed by Nature for the resort of the invalid – the very spot which Thousands seemed in need of – the most desirable distance from London! One complete, measured mile nearer than East Bourne. Only conceive, sir, the advantage of saving a whole mile in a long journey. But Brinshore, sir, which I dare say you have in your eye – the attempts of two or three speculating people about Brinshore this last year, to raise that paltry hamlet, lying as it does between a stagnant marsh, a bleak moor and the constant effluvia of a ridge of putrifying sea weed, can end in nothing but their own disappointment. What in the name of common sense is to *recommend* Brinshore? A most insalubrious air – roads proverbially detestable – water brackish beyond example – impossible to get a good dish of tea within three miles of the place – and as for the soil, it is so cold and ungrateful that it can hardly be made to yield a cabbage. Depend upon it, sir, that this is a faithful description of Brinshore – not in the smallest degree exaggerated – and if you have heard it differently spoken of –'

'Sir, I never heard it spoken of in my life before,' said Mr Heywood. 'I did not know there was such a place in the world.'

'You did not! There, my dear (turning with exultation to his wife) – you see how it is. So much for the celebrity of Brinshore! This gentleman did not know there was such a place in the world.'

Jane Austen; Sanditon *(1817)*

Sussex by the Sea

In the churchyard of South Bersted lie the graves of Sir Richard Hotham, the founder of nearby Bognor Regis, and William Ward Higgs, a Victorian composer now known for nothing but the stirring tune which is played at practically every Sussex event which requires music. The words are much less well known, and for good reason, but here's the chorus.

For we're the men from Sussex, Sussex by the Sea.
We plough and sow and reap and mow,
And useful men are we;
And when you go to Sussex,
Whoever you may be,
You may tell them all that we stand or fall
For Sussex by the Sea !
Oh Sussex, Sussex by the Sea !
Good old Sussex by the Sea !
You may tell them all that we stand or fall,
For Sussex by the Sea

William Ward Higgs; 'Sussex by the Sea'

Entertainers on the Prom

There was plenty of music. There were German bands and regular military bands and hurdy-gurdy men with their monkeys, blind accordionists and one-armed fiddlers, harpists, one-man bands and players on the spoons, harmonium players, unaccompanied singers and Ethiopian serenaders. Add to these the stilt-walkers, the wrestlers, the street acrobats, the men who juggled barrels with their feet, the fire-eaters and the conjurors, the escapologists and chapeauologists who, by a turn or two of the brim of their felt hats, became the Emperor Napoleon or a highwayman or a lady of the streets or a country bumpkin. There were ventriloquists and performing dogs. There were even dogs that told fortunes – dogs clever enough, according to their masters, to tell your future from the cards. Italian women at Hastings trained birds in cages to perform similar tricks.

Tom Kemp, who kept a live crocodile in his bath as part of his act, performed on Brighton's West Pier for many years in the 1920s and 1930s. His routine with the sausages was said to be unsurpassed. On Worthing pier in the 1950s Gordon Hamilton gave eighteen ten-minute Punch and Judy shows every day. And Percy Press – 'Uncle Percy' to countless children for thirty years from 1951 at the White Rock – was probably the best known of all the Punch and Judy men. All of these voices call out over the decades, urging the visitors to join in the fun, to listen to the music, to give the 'bottler' a copper or two, to come onto the West Pier to see Professor Doughty and his Performing Dogs or Professor Powsey diving off the same pier while mounted on a bicycle. Or why not at Hastings watch G.W. Houghton, billed as the Human Torpedo, performing 'one of the most difficult feats ever attempted'? Houghton would offer a challenge to the world. He would wager £25 that he would propel his body a full 33 yards 15 inches in the sea with his head totally immersed. Or why not, between the wars, respond to Biddy Stonham, the Hastings tubman? His encouragement, especially to young ladies, to join him in a seaborne tub regularly worked and Biddy, his black top hat decked with flowers, would sit his uncertain passenger in the tub and then would balance on the rim, twisting round the tub until it overturned and all parties fell into the water.

W.H. *Johnson;* Seaside Entertainment in Sussex *(2001)*

Shipwrecks as History

One of the greatest known concentrations of historic sunken ships lies off the shore of south-east England, particularly where it borders the English Channel, one of the busiest seaways in the world. The enormous wealth of historical informatin preserved in these wrecks in incalculable, and they form part of the 'new frontier' of archaeological exploration – underwater.

Ships are the buildings of the sea, and it is by studying their surviving remains as wrecks that we can better understand and illustrate the history of mankind's long association with the sea. This is particularly so in th south-east region where there is an exceptional shoreline concentration of historic shipwrecks that can be visited by

non-divers at suitable low tides. It lies in East Sussex between
Camber in the east an Cuckmere Haven, just west of Beachy Head in
the west, where there are prserved the substantial remains of large
ships of the seventeenth, eighteenth, nineteenth and twentieth
centuries. This range of age for ships visible at low tide has no known
parallel in Britain, and may be unique in Europe. Visitors can trace in
at least seven wrecks the development of ships from wood and sail to
steel and engine. The extraordinary nature of this group is underlined
by the fact that two of the three protected historic wreck sites that are
visible at low tide in the whole of the British Isles, lie in this area.
Peter Marsden; The Historic Shipwrecks of South-East England *(1987)*

Looters

Sussex men that dwell upon the shore
Look out when storms arise and billows roar;
Devoutly praying with uplifted hands
That some well-laden ship may strike the sands,
To whose rich cargo they may make pretence
And fatten on the spoils of Providence.
William Congreve; Epilogue to 'The Mourning Bride'

Every beach in Sussex has claimed its victims. This was the fate of the
Nympha Americana, one of the most spectacular wrecks on the
Sussex coast. When she was wrecked in November 1747 she split in
two and [a] contemporary print . . . shows the stern remarkably
undamaged standing proud on the beach. She was rumoured to have
a rich cargo and within hours the beach was crowded with villagers
eager to see what they could salvage from the wreck. Troops were
called out to control the crowd and two men were shot dead. A
macabre touch is that the weather at the time was exceptionally cold
and some people died of exposure on the beach, one report
numbering them at fifty.

The *Nympha Americana* did indeed have a rich cargo. She had
been captured off Cadiz by English privateers at the very beginning
of her voyage to Vera Cruz, loaded with mercury – used in the

refining of gold and silver – bales of cloth and gold. So organised was the privateering trade at this time that she was taken into Lisbon for insurance to be arranged in London before starting her voyage to England. She stopped off at Portsmouth and was on the final leg of her journey to London when she was wrecked. On hearing of the wreck one of the members of the privateering synicate went straight to the Secretary of State for a warrant authorising him to use troops to control looters and hurried to Crowlink to safeguard their property. Enough of the cargo was salvaged to raise £39,000 when it was auctioned at Lewes, leaving the insurance company to pay £117,000 in compensation.

Just over a year later there was another spectacular shipwreck near Hastings when the *Amsterdam* East Indiaman was driven ashore at Bulverhythe after a horrendous eighteen-day voyage from Holland. The brand-new ship had been repeatedly delayed by bad weather before finally setting sail on 8 January 1749. She immediately ran into headwinds and fifty crew members died, probably from a tropical disease, as she clawed her way down Channel.

Opposite the Sussex coast the wind rose to gale force and the captain decided to seek shelter in Pevensey Bay, where the ship struck a reef which carried away the rudder. Unable to steer, the captain dropped anchor off Bexhill and prepared to ride out the storm. But the crew, who had been battened down in their quarters throughout the storm, broke into the liquor store and demanded that the ship be run ashore, which the captain did, firing the guns to alert the local inhabitants.

As usual at a wreck hundreds of people turned up to see what they could loot, and it is reported that the soldiers took their turn in plundering it themselves. What became of the crew is not known in detail. . . . Forty, who were sick, were taken off the ship the day after she beached and those who died were buried in the graveyard of Bulverhythe church and that of St Andrew's, Hastings.

The *Amsterdam* had gone ashore on quicksand, and as attempts were made to salvage the remainder of the cargo she gradually sank into the beach. The salvagers were unable to open the hatches, in spite of lighting fires around them and attempting to blow them open with gunpowder – during which the engineer, Christopher Nutt, was killed by an accidental explosion – and after a month the ship had sunk thirteen feet. Ten days later she was five feet further down and salvage attempts were abandoned. There she stayed until 1969 when work began on a new sewer outfall at Bulverhythe and it was decided to escavate the wreck. Some of the items recovered can be seen at the Shipwreck Heritage Centre at Hastings.

David Harries; Maritime Sussex *(1997)*

A Lifeboat Disaster

Arthur Mee covered the country in order to write his colourful guides, and the Sussex volume is typical in the brio of its entries. The terrible story he tells here is of the worst lifeboat disaster in British history, the loss of the Mary Stanford *in November 1928.*

A furious gale was sweeping the Channel. It had borne the ship *Alice of Riga* on to the shallows halfway between Rye and Dungeness.

A message to Rye Harbour told the news an hour before the late November dawn, and in the darkness and the gale the lifeboat put out with 17 men. Only men without fear, or with the courage that defies it, would have dared to put out in that raging sea.

The watchers saw the *Mary Stanford* and her crew labouring through the heavy seas. They disappeared, and were never there seen again till the lifeboat was washed ashore, bottom upward, and the bodies of the harbour men followed her.

Scrap by scrap the tale of what happened was gathered in. The *Alice*, though driven into the shallows near the Camber Sands, was not at once broken up, or even helpless. The German steamer *Smyrna* got near her and took off her crew, landing them afterwards safely at Dover.

This news was known a few minutes after the lifeboat had set out. It was telephoned to the lifeboat station, and rockets were sent to recall her. Her crew, battling with the mounting seas, could never have seen them. The lifeboat went on. It went on till it reached the abandoned *Alice*. Its task, its courage, had all been in vain. The ship was empty. The *Mary Stanford* and her crew now had to fight for their own lives.

The gale abated none of its fury. For more than five hours they fought it. They were fighting it still when those on the shore saw the lifeboat a mile away, coming home. A mile away, but a mile of raging sea. As every eye was strained to watch the lifeboat she luched under a fiercer gust; her mast went over the side; she was borne over; she was gone. None would ever reach the shore alive.

Arthur Mee; The King's England: Sussex (1937)

A Sailor's Memorial

George Ragless of South Bersted drowned off Bognor in a storm on May 23 1867 aged 21 years, and this verse with its rocking rhythms was carved on his gravestone.

> Brought up from his youth on the billow,
> He sailed o'er the fathomless deep,
> And now the cold earth is his pillow
> And sound and unroken his sleep.
> Here no winds and now waves overtake him
> No tempests can ever arise
> But the voice of the Saviour shall wake him
> And bid him ascend to the skies.

'Horsing' at Chichester

The garfish is a lamb of the sea. He is never tired of gambolling, and this spirit of *joi de vivre* often leads to his undoing.

Garfish follow the whitebait shoals, but when not pursuing their prey they hunt around for straggling flotsam in the shape of sticks, paper bags or small pieces of wreckage on the surface; then the fun begins. Silvery bodies flash in the sunlight as they spring from side to side of any object which catches their eye. All thought of food is forgotten as they follow the floating debris, leaping, twisting and turning.

When the garfish are known to have arrived the fishermen go 'horsing'. This is a colloquial and rather obscure name for a remarkable method of reaping the harvest of the sea. The men cut branches of withy sticks, to which are tied lengths of string. These are stowed in the boat and with a skeine or long net abroad the fishers set off. When the garfish are sighted the sticks are distributed over the water and kept in position by the mooring lines. Usually the anxious watchers have not long to wait before the fish indulge in their passion for gymnastics. When the performance is in full progress the net is shot and many sad and disillusioned fish appear in the market.

This interesting method has been practised in Chichester Harour from time immemorial.

Grey mullet are perhaps the most difficult to capture with a net. Instead of making a blind rush for the bag of the net when drawn into the shallows, they nose about in a most methodical manner, and if no outlet presents itself they leap to freedom over the cork-line like greyhounds over hurdles.

To outwit their quarry the fishermen adopt many methods. Some, when grey mullet are known to be in the net, beat the water frantically with an oar, others wade waist deep, making the welkin ring with shouts and oaths in an endeavour to prevent the fish from leaping.

But perhaps the most ingenious scheme was that of an old fisherman at Emsworth, who trained a Labrador retriever to swim constantly round the incoming net. Thus, between the net, the dog and the deep sea the mullet were forced to passive resistance.

R. *Thurston Hopkins*, Small Sailing Craft *(1931)*

Counting the Catch

The counting of the catch when a herring boat comes in at Hastings is interesting both for the way in which it is done and the quaint terms still in use as they were on the same spot centuries ago.

The fish are thrown out on the beach before counting, the man who does the latter being known as the 'teller'. Taking the herrings up four at a time (two in each hand), this number being described as a 'warp', he throws them into baskets hoding a bushel each and known as 'prickles'. Each warp thrown into the basket is counted 'one, two three,' 'one and twenty', 'two and twenty', and so on up to sixty-six, when the 'teller' calls out 'score'.

The 'scorer' (another man) repeats 'score', at the same time making an upright chalk mark upon the bow, or some other part of the boat, which is drawn up on the beach alongside. Until a few years ago the ancient method of cutting a notch in a piece of wood, or 'tally', for each score recorded was used.

The sixty-six 'warps' or 264 herrings, are counted as two hundred. When 1,000 is reached the scorer draws a line from the top of the fourth stroke to the bottom of the first. The fish are sold by the 'last', understood to be 10,000 fish, but actually over 13,000, so the buyer gets a good many thrown in. All reckoning is done in 'warps' – i.e. four fish.

The weather terms used by the fishermen are also very curious, and as old as the ancient town itself.

Salty weather with a heaving, oily sea is called 'swallocky' and is generally known to presage a storm, but a dead calm with close moist air is described as 'planety' weather. A scattered mass of cirrus cloud in the form of a loop is given the quaint name of 'eddenbite', whose derivation is hard to guess. Other white clouds blown by the wind are 'windogs' and 'messengers'. Small low clouds in an otherwise clear sky are 'port-boys'.

A mock sun, always taken as an ominous portent, is described as 'smither diddles', and two kinds of hail are recognised, possibly ordinary hail and sleet, the latter being given the comical name of 'egger-nogger'. Changeable, unsettled weather is described as 'shucky', and what the ordinary seaman would call real 'dirty' weather the Hastings fisherman will call 'truggy'.

Eva Bretherton; The Sussex County Magazine, (1927)

3 · ALL IN A DAY'S WORK

Work occupies so much of our lives that it demands to be represented in our anthology, however randomly. We begin with the labour a smith owed his lord, the Archbishop of Canterbury, on the manor of Tangmere in 1285.

A Smith's Feudal Duties

John Marscal holds half a virgate and owes yearly, omitting Christmas and Whitsun, 100 works. And he shall thresh 1 measure of corn of which 4 make a bushel for one work, and thresh two measures of barley or pease retch, or beans or 1 quarter of oats for one work. He shall break clods or hoe from daylight until nones for 1 work. He shall ditch 32 feet in length and 1 spit deep for 1 work and as much he shall make of them hedge for 1 work. He shall ditch 16 feet in length, 4 feet in width and 2 spits in depth for 1 work. He shall mow with other tenants the meadow of Ersnyre and shall have his bundle of hay. He shall make hay with the others in that meadow and the lord shall give them 12d. He shall mow two meadows in Wodemed for 7 days and on Westmede for 2 or 3 days until it is reped, and what is mown in 2 days there he shall make with his companions . . . and the lord shall give the mowers of the two meadows 4s for making the hay. He shall enclose in the field 32 feet length of fencing which he shall cut and gather in the park for 1 work. He shall put 1 row of dung on 1 furlong for 2 works. He shall spread a row for 1 work. He shall carry a carload of hay from the park for 1 work, and 2 cartloads of hay from Westmede for 1 work. He shall plough a strip in winter and another strip in spring without harrowing and without counting a work. He shall do carrying service on alternate Saturdays at Louyngton or elsewhere within the mannor, without counting it a work, and she shall carry to Midhurst, Arundel or Emmesworth, that is to the bridge at those places, without counting it a work. He shall make half a seam of malt for one work and the lord shall provide firewood. And if in carrying he is delayed out for the night it will count two works. He shall make 1 quarter o flour and when he carries the flour to the house he shall have his food. He shall provide 2 men at the harvest boonwork at the lords food and if he has a plough he shall plough 1 acre as a boon work. He cannot marry himself or marry his sons or daughters without leave, nor sell for himself a foal he has foaled, if maile. And after his death the lord shall have his best ox or cow, and if there be neither he shall have 5s. And his widow shall pay relief and shall remain in the said tenement undisturbed, doing the services.

From John Lowerson; A Short History of Sussex (1980)

Farm Labour

A glimpse of the old Sussex field routine, not greatly changed in the remote districts today, was given to Mr Gordon thirty years ago by an aged labourer. This was the day:

'Out in the morning at four o'clock. Mouthful of bread and cheese and pint of ale. Then off to the harvest field. Rippin and moen (reaping and mowing) till eight. Then morning brakfast and small beer. Brakfast – a piece of fat pork as thick as your hat is wide. Then work till ten o'clock: then a mouthful of bread and cheese and a pint of strong beer. ('Farnooner,' i.e. forenooner; 'farnooner's lunch' we called it.) Work till twelve. Then at dinner in the farmhouse; sometimes a leg of mutton, sometimes a piece of ham and plum pudding. Then work till five, then a *nunch* and a quart of ale. Nunch was cheese, 'twas skimmed cheese though. Then work till sunset, then home and have supper and a pint of ale. I never knew a man drunk in the harvest field in my life. Could drink six quarts, and believe that a man might drink two gallons in a day. All of us were in the house (i.e. the usual hired servants, and those specially engaged for the harvest): the yearly servants used to go with the monthly ones.

'There were two thrashers, and the head thrasher used always to go before the reapers. A man could cut according to the goodness of the job, half-an-acre a day. The terms of wages were £3.10 to 50s for the month.

'When the hay was in cock or the wheat in shock, then the Titheman come; you didn't dare take up a field without you let him know. If the Titheman didn't come at the time, you tithed yourself. He marked his sheaves with a bough or bush. You couldn't get over the Titheman. If you began at a hedge and made the tenth cock smaller than the rest, the Titheman might begin in the middle just where he liked. The Titheman at Harting, old John Blackmore, lived at Mundy's. His grandson is blacksmith at Harting now. All the tithing was quiet. You didn't dare even set your eggs till the Titheman had been and ta'en his tithe. The usual day's work was from 7 to 5.'

E. V. Lucas; Highways and Byways of Sussex (1935)

The Lure of the Shepherd's Work

Barclay Wills escaped the life of a London clerk ('My sketch-book and binoculars saved me from the hopeless futility of suburban life') to become a shopkeeper in Brighton, close to his beloved Downs. He was to write several books about rural life in Sussex, including a number about the work of his friends, the downland shepherds.

So each year passes, and the shepherd carries on, working seven days a week. In return for such devotion he receives a wage which other workers would despise. I have known a farmer to say: 'I wouldn't part with old Mike; no matter when I go by, early or late, weekday or Sunday, he is always about, looking after the sheep!' Perhaps he imagined that old Mike worked simply to please him, but it was not so. Such work is not all done for the sake of the farmer, for if the shepherd moved to another farm he would do just the same. It is the lure of his craft which causes him to put his dumb families before everything else, and to stay with them for many an extra hour in order to give a 'last look round' for their benefit.

Many references have been made in print to the lives of shepherds, and many opinions expressed concerning their outlook on life. If we were able to interview all the old Sussex shepherds at this date we should probably find that the majority of them view the changes and ways of modern times with a certain amount of disfavour. They are forced to adapt themselves to new conditions and move with the times to some extent, but the habits of a lifetime (in many cases strengthened by hereditary tendencies) are not easily altered.

My hours spent with shepherds at all seasons of the year have been a revelation in many ways. My own early idea of a shepherd as a man, crook in hand, with nothing to do but to watch his flock, was soon exploded. Gradually I sorted out the many little tangled lines of thought that occurred to me; gradually I traced the reason for some action or for the careful attention given to some little detail, and every fact I gleaned pointed backwards – back on through the years to the days when the shepherd learned his craft, and sometimes further still, to the time of his parents and grandparents. One old man explained a point thus: 'My gran'father did it thet way, an' my father did it thet way, an' now I doos it the same. There be a right way an' a wrong way o' doin' things, an' the sooner you learns to do a thing the right way the better it be for ye, for then yew see yew doos it right wi'out thinkin' 'bout it.'

Many of the oldest shepherds now living started work at a very early age. They absorbed the details of their craft at a date when the craze for speed was unknown; when, as one old man remarked to me, 'the farmer shared the shepherd's pride and delight in the flock, and in all the shepherd did.' That is why we still find old men doing more than a young man would expect to do for the wages paid. With experience of duties gained as shepherd boy, teg boy and under-shepherd grew that pride which was shared by the farmer – a pride which even extended to the bells used on the flock.

How different it is today! The craze for speed has affected everybody. Ways have changed; good manners are old-fashioned; thoroughness is out of date; the old shepherd himself is out of date; few care tuppence about his thoroughness or his pride in his work; his only enjoyment is in the thought of past days when he was 'somebody', and so any old shepherd you meet is usually quiet and reticent until he discovers whether your interest is genuine. If he is satisfied you soon know; he responds to enquiries, but he is like a dormouse waking up in Spring, for at the touch of memory's hand his attitude changes, his stiffness relaxes, his eyes are young again, and as he talks for a little while he becomes 'somebody' once more!

Do not despise an old shepherd because he appears to be simple; his simplicity is actually a sign of strength. He may not fit in with modern ideas, but it must be remembered that when he started with an inborn love for one kind of work he was first taught obedience, correctness, thoroughness, self-reliance and untiring devotion to the flock. As shepherd he became a man of importance and ruled his own little kingdom. The drawbacks attending his job were long hours, the many inconveniences resulting from unkind weather, and the low wages; but there were compensations in other ways. His rather hard upbringing helped him tackle every task in a methodical manner, without unnecessary worry, and his solitary peaceful hours in the open air gradually cast a spell over him – a spell so strong that at last he developed this quiet, simple manner. Hidden under his cloak is a wonderful love for the freedom of open spaces, for pictures of sheep on the hillside and in the fold, for fields of mangold and rape, for the familiar starlings and the hundred and one items which he meets and notes as he goes to and fro.

Barclay Wills; Shepherds of Sussex (1934)

Yer Own Back

In my local radio days I was lucky beyond measure to meet Bert Winborne, a gardener of the old school who became a regular 'on air' and a good friend. He died in 2002 at the age of 97, and is much missed.

When we wanted something extra we'd get a builder in to take the big slab off the old cesspit, and we'd dig the sludge from that into the garden. It used to be done on a moonlit night when it was frosty, and that helped to keep the smell down.

There was a crust about a foot deep, and we cut it out and took the pieces up into the shed to dry out. Then we'd beat them up with a big old wooden beater and that was shovelled again into wheelbarrows and taken to the potting shed and put under the bench in a big bin.

We had a name for it. It was called 'Yer Own Back'. The head gardener knew the best mixtures to use for everything, and he'd tell you so much leaf soil (there was no peat in those days) and how many handfuls of Own Back if you were potting stuff on. It wasn't a joke. That's what it was called.

The early peas liked it, too. We used to grow them in the greenhouse, and we'd give them a shake of this dry sludge each side of them and draw it up with a broad hoe, and that used to give them a bit of colouring. By Jove, we used to get some peas!

Once that was off we'd have long scoops and bodges – tanks on wheels – and we used to fill them up, run them round the garden and tip them up on the ground. Then we'd lime everywhere to keep the pong down.

It certainly put plenty of lime and iron in the ground and, you know, we could grow just about anything in that old sludge.

Bert Winborne in David Arscott; The Upstart Gardener (1986)

A Farrier's Life

Susan Rowland specialises in publishing the memories of 'ordinary' working people in the Lewes area, among them Frank Dean. Several generations of his family have worked at the forge in Rodmell.

My training was given to me entirely by my father. He was a first class farrier and blacksmith. He'd show you how to do a job, but was very loth to let you take over the major role. The first horse I ever shod was when father was not well. One had a shoe off and the carter brought it in. I said to him, 'You know father is laid up.' 'Yes,' he said, 'but you've helped him ever so many times, you've seen him do it, and I have got to have him shod.' So I put that shoe on, and before father got back to work I had another one to do all round. Since that day I've never left off shoeing.

We've been doing Plumpton and Brighton Race Meetings for quite a lot of years; the South of England Show at Ardingly; and the International Show Jumping Course at Hickstead for about 30 years. Racehorses are shod with aluminium or lightweight steel plates, the old maxim being that 'an ounce off the hoof is worth a pound off the back'. I am still registered to shoe, but these days I only do emergencies. At the end of last summer a horse travelling the South Downs Way lost two shoes, so I made a pair and put them on the old cob.

People sometimes ask me if I have ever been kicked by a horse. I always reply 'Not if I could help it!' On the whole you don't get kicked because your skill keeps you away. One of my father's favourite sayings was 'Never stand behind a horse or in front of a judge'.

Frank Dean; Strike while the iron's hot (1994)

Warring Postcard Manufacturers

An energetic tussle between business rivals in the summer of 1904 occupied the pages of the Hastings and St Leonards Observer. *I'm indebted to postcard collector Dave Kibble for bringing this little spat to my attention. Croyle's has long since gone, but Judge's prosper to this day.*

June 11, 1904
Judge's Postcards:
'LIGHTNING' POSTCARDS. WARNING!
Our photographic postcard 'Lightning at Hastings' taken on Monday night June 6th is copyright.

It having come to our knowledge that pirate copies are on the market, this is to give notice that unless the sale of such be stopped legal proceedings will be taken.

None Genuine Unless Stamped 'Fred Judge'.

THE SALE OF THIS ONE POSTCARD ALONE IN 3 DAYS EXCEEDED 2,000 COPIES.

Angus Croyle:
Lightning Postcards

LEGAL OPINION
'Others not to be Compared'
CROYLE WAS THE ORIGINATOR OF 'LIGHTNING' POSTCARDS.

June 18
Judge's:
'Lightning at Hastings', taken on June 6th 1904 – the Latest
addition to the 'JUDGE' SERIES of REAL PHOTOGRAPHIC POSTCARDS. The
number of this one Card made and sold to date now exceeds 5,000.
Croyle:
The UNIVERSAL OPINION is that Croyle's 'LIGHTNING' POSTCARDS are
the best ever seen. Over 7,500 sold.

July 9
Judge's:
The sale of our postcard, 'Lightning at Hastings', taken on June 6th
this year, now considerably exceeds 10,000.

July 16
Croyle:
TO ANYONE WHO CAN PROVE that my are not genuine I will give £100
reward. ANGUS N. CROYLE, The Originator of Genuine 'Lightning'
Postcards. To be obtained only at 11 Norman Road, St Leonards-
on-Sea.

July 30
Judge's:
Number of copies of our Lightning Postcard sold in seven weeks
exceeds 13,000.
JUDGE'S PHOTO STORES, 21A Wellington Place, Hastings

August 20
Croyle:
Everyone should secure at once a copy of my latest Copyright
'LIGHTNING' POSTCARDS Which is the most wonderful EVER
PRODUCED.

A Brighton Cabbie

QueenSpark Books in Brighton are another publisher to be commended for recording the lives of local people. This memoir dates from around 1926.

Taxi driving in those days was totally different from the saloon cars now. Most of them were all open in the front, just a roof, windscreen and, if you were lucky, you had what was called side curtains.

In the winter it was terrible. The icy wind when you were going along would almost cut your ears and nose off. When it rained your right shoulder would be soaked through, right to the skin. Perhaps, while standing in the rank waiting for a fare, it would start snowing and you'd have to put a rug over the radiator, and my feet would be like blocks of ice. It was worse than awful. Perhaps, after waiting for nearly an hour or more, some old girl would come along and say 'Dudley Hotel' – 500 yards away – and give you eighteen pence: that was 1s 4d for the fare and tuppence for yourself. The old car, with starting her up and keeping her warm and going to the hotel, would use almost a gallon of petrol. So I'd get about 4d out of it.

Of course, like everything else, it was not all bad. I had some wonderful days' takings, and my first Christmas in 1926 I had a wonderful holiday. I worked right through it! I worked Christmas Eve, Christmas Day, Boxing Day, right up to the Sunday. It snowed all Boxing Day and I never stopped running. As fast as I dropped one fare, either I picked one up there or a little further on. It went like that for two or three days.

My father did well also. I gave him some of my takings and put £10 in my Post Office account, paid the insurance and licence and garage for a week. It was a shilling a night, and six bob a week if you paid for a week. One month cost me 24s, quite a lot of money in those days. I paid, because I knew business would be bad for weeks after, and it was bad. One day I pulled onto Brunswick Place at nine in the morning about three weeks after Christmas. I stopped there all day until 9pm without turning a wheel. I never even went and got a cup of tea in case I missed a fare. I ran to the lavatory and back. All to no avail, since not one fare came along. Yet over the other side there were two taxis who did fairly well.

I eventually pulled off at 9pm, went down to Divals and ordered two rashers, two fried eggs, bubble and squeak, four or five slices, and after that I had some bread pudding and two or three cups of tea. The girl who served me was a girl I knew, and when she asked if I was hungry, I said no, I was just having a snack!

When I told her that I had had nothing to eat since breakfast, and that I had stood on the rank all day without moving, she said I must have been barmy to do such a thing. I said so, too, and vowed there and then that, wherever I was, and whatever the circumstances, I would always get my dinner and tea and never do anything like that again.

Bert Healey; Hard Times & Easy Terms (1980)

A Close Shave

Bob Copper has written some wonderful books, rich in detail, about growing up in Rottingdean. Here he tells of an incident when, as a young barber doing 'outside work', he visited the Collins family.

'I'm glad you come t'day,' she went on, 'it'll tidy the ol' chep up a bit. The relatives come down t'morrer.' There was a pause while we sipped our cups. 'The funeral's on Tuesday.'

The kettle was beginning to sing and wisps of steam started to curl lazily from its spout. 'The funeral?' I asked. The conversation had taken an unexpected turn and I hadn't the slightest notion what she was talking about. She drained her teacup and put it in the saucer on the table. 'Yes,' she said, picking tea leaves from the tip of her tongue, 'he died yest'dy aft'noon.'

The kettle burst into spluttering life, the tin lid rattled like a kettle drum and water spewed out on to the embers, sending clouds of steam up the chimney and billowing into the room.

'Died?' I said, as she took the kettle and stood it in the hearth, and my voice sounded faint and far away, as if it was coming through a long tunnel and the blood began to pound like a hammer in my temples.

'Yes,' she said in a matter of fact tone, collecting the empty teacups, 'a very peaceful end. Your water's ready, look.'

I took the handle with the kettle-holder and filled my shaving mug. I seemed to have lost control of the situation and was being carried away on a tidal wave of events with no power to stop it. Surely she didn't expect me to shave . . .

'Ah well, I'll leave you to it then,' she said, going out of the back door into the yard. The wave was beginning to curl and the surf crashed about my head. There was no going back now.

'You'd better take a candle,' she called. 'I've pulled the bedroom blind down and you mustn't let it up agin out o' respect f' the dead. He has been laid out.'

I delayed the lighting of the candle for as long as I could, but my fumbling fingers found difficulty in striking the match anyway. What could I do? Apart from moving as slowly as possible to put off the dreadful moment, I could see no way of averting my fate. I remembered having read somewhere that an old negress with commendable philosophy once said, 'Some troubles is so little that you can step over 'em. Some a little bigger you can usually step round. But some is so durned big all you can do is duck your head and go wadin' right on into 'em.' And so it seemed with me at that moment.

I donned my white coat and, taking the case and the shaving mug in one hand and the candle-stick in the other, walked with leaden feet up the narrow, creaking stairway. The stair-carpet was worn into harp-strings at the edges of the treads and the brass stair-rods reflected the orange light of the candle. My heart bumped slowly up behind me – stair by stair. Up on the landing, I stood for a moment before lifting the latch on his bedroom door and going in.

Pulling the white sheet back from his head I saw the old familiar face fixed in the horrifying, waxwork mask of death. I went about my task mechanically while my mind flitted about among the crowded memories I had of old 'Buck' in life. The puckish humour, the glint of schoolboy mischief in his eyes which now stared sightlessly at the ceiling. The beer-sodden jokes when he had staggered into the saloon one day, carrying a potted plant describing it as 'a spiraea or lemmin plaant', and not knowing whether he wanted 'a sh–, shave or shampoo'. I recalled his cryptic comment on the edge of my razor once in reply to the customary enquiry: 'Wal, bwoy,' he had said, 'if I kin kip from cryin', that bugger'll stop me from laughin'.'

Now I was thinking sadly that, even if the razor did pull, poor Buck wouldn't feel it, and wondering why the pressure of my fingertip on his cold cheek left a depression that was slow to fill and whether or not he would bleed if I cut him. It was a traumatic moment, macabre and pathetic, and I was torn between repugnance and sympathy. When I had finished, I pulled the sheet back over his head with a slight shudder and went downstairs in a dream.

Bob Copper; *Early to Rise* (1976)

The First Tractor

Sussex farms must have been tranquil places seventy years ago. This is a memory of Banks Farm, Barcombe, then owned by Hart Vercoe.

In 1935 old Mr Vercoe was persuaded to buy a tractor. He ordered a Standard Fordson from Haywards Heath costing about one hundred and fifty pounds, but he died a month before it was delivered in April. By coincidence, as the tractor arrived one of the older horses, Traveller, went lame and had to be destroyed. This left us with Captain, Blossom and Boxer, but they were not needed so much with the arrival of the tractor. Mr Vercoe's fifteen year old grandson, who lived with them in the farmhouse, was taught to drive the tractor by a man who came down from the works for a week. Then I had to teach him how to plough. We had a trailer plough in those days. At the end of the summer, about October time, the tractor was put to bed for the winter. This was the practice on most farms as you didn't want them on the ground when it was wet. I carried on through the winter with the horses.

In March of the following spring Alan Vercoe offered me the job of driving the tractor, saying he would get someone else to drive the horses if I agreed. I didn't know the first thing about the tractor except that you wound it up at the front and steered it with a wheel. I was really 'green', having only ever worked with horses. I didn't know the first thing about engines. I wasn't sure what to do when he offered me the job. I told him I would have to think about it as I had a small family by then, three children, and needed to talk it over with my wife. People were getting tractors as they were becoming more plentiful – Cornwells had two by that time. I said to Elsie, 'The way I see it is the tractor's going to take the place of the horse. I think I ought to take the job while I've got the chance.' She said 'Will it mean you won't get so much money?' I replied, 'No it won't, because if it does I shan't take it.' When I saw Mr Vercoe again he said 'What do you think about the job?' I said, 'Look, I've got a small family, so I can't take a lower wage. There won't be so many hours to do if I haven't got the horses to look after.' 'Oh no,' he said, 'I'll pay you the same money. I never expected you to take a cut in wages.'

So I became a tractor driver. It was a Fordson tractor, on cleats to give a grip. Although it didn't do road work as such, there was quite a bit of road to go up and down to the fields. They were still made of flint and wore down the cleats, which soon had to be replaced. Cleats go across the wheel at a diagonal angle. They were made of metal and bolted on. When they were worn we used to get wheel spin, so Mr Vercoe brough some spade lugs for me to fit on. These bolted on straight across the wheel using the front hole of one cleat and the back hole of the one in front.

I spent my first three days tractor driving pulling a cultivator, then I had to go poughing out in Line Field, by the railway. It was a trailer plough which was operated by pulling a cord to trip and lift it up when turning. Pulling the cord again dropped it back into the ground. Late in the afternoon I got to where there was a farm crossing gate. This was ten feet wide and allowed wagons to cross the railway line. I pulled the cord and tripped the plough and must have hung on to it too long, for it tripped again and went back down. I felt the tractor pull again and wondered why. When I looked round I was just a few inches from the gate, but the tractor wheel had gone through. I managed to stop saying 'Wo!', as I would have done if I'd had the horses. I tripped the plough and backed out, noticing that I had broken three slats on the gate. Half an hour later the old ganger on the line came by, probably going home to tea.

'Harry,' I said, 'I've had a mishap.'

'Oh dear,' he replied. 'have you got any slats up at the farm that would go in there.'

'Yes, I think we have. There is an old broken white gate up there.'

'Well, you bring me down three or four bits and I'll mend it. Then I'll leave it a little while before I report it and we'll get a new gate.' Which is exactly what he did.

Harold Cannings; Follow the plough *(1992)*

A Frosty Reception

David Atkins gave up a working life in the City to try his hand at running an apple orchard in West Sussex. He experienced many ups and downs. This extract describes lighting deisel-filled pots in the orchards as means of keeping the frost at bay. The reference in the verse at the end is to the old Sussex saying 'Wunt be druv' – the native's legendary, and commendable, refusal to bend the knee.

When the temperature dropped to the right degree at the lowest point we would start to light. We knocked off the lids of each pot, dropped in the lighted petrol and then on to the next pot. Four thousand pots take quite a lot of lighting. In order to save diesel we would light alternate pots in the hope that these would hold the frost. It sometimes did. On other nights the thermometers spaced all across the orchards would show a brief upswing when we lit and then down they would plunge again, until in the end every fire was ablaze. Our doctor, returning late at night from a call, remembers seeing the whole of our hill aflame. It was a lovely sight among the blossom.

When the frost broke through our defences I felt much as I did when the German army broke through behind us in 1940. It was a feeling of sick despair; all that effort wasted and how would the farm survive?

As the sky lightened and as last the great yellow sun came edging over Toat hill, we would continue the ceaseless patrol of the thermometers. This was the most dangerous moment and on some night we would still be lighting one hour after dawn. At last the temperature would edge up and now one could see the frost on every leaf and bud. Had we or had we not held the temperature to that vital last degree? A flower is either killed or it lives. A tenth of a degree may make all the difference.

Now we had the job of putting out the lamps, and this one did by slamming the lid hard on the funnel. Nine times out of ten this would work, but, after one had passed, some lamps would burst into flame again with a thump. Before the final lamp was extinguished the other staff had come on duty and at last one could go home to a bath and breakfast.

Several nights of frost left one's nerves on edge. One of our best girls remarked on the bad frost damage and asked if I'd seen it.

'Of course I bloody have,' I snarled at her.

Next day she handed me an envelope. In it was a short poem.

I did not bring the horrid frost
Or jump about with glee.
I do my job and mun be druv,
So don't you shout at me.

I apologised and she is still with us many years later.

David Atkins; The Cuckoo in June *(1992)*

4 · CHURCH AND CHAPEL

Religion has brought its torments as well as its consolations to Sussex, publicly and privately, as this chapter reveals. We begin with the grant of land to St Wilfrid, the great northern bishop who began the spread of Christianity throughout Sussex. This document is almost certainly a forgery well after the event, made by the Church to protect a property claim which was nevertheless genuine: it was King Aethelwealh, married to a Christian wife, who is thought to have granted the land to Wilfrid to finance his missionary work.

St Wilfrid's Grant

AD 683
Grant by Aaedwalla, king of Wessex,
to Bishop Wilfrid of land at Selsey &c

In the name of our Saviour Jesus Christ! We have brought nothing into this world and it is certain we can carry nothing out. Therefore the eternal and heavenly rewards of the Kingdom on high are to be sought instead of earthly and transitory things.

On that account, I Caedwalla, king by the grace of God, have been asked by the venerable Bishop Wilfrid to be so good as to grant him a little land for the support of the followers of Christ who lead a monastic life, and for the construction of a monastery on the place which is called Selsey. In addition I will give in his own power of gift the land which is called Aldingbourne and Lidsey, of 6 hides; and 6 at

Westergate, and 8 at Mundham, and 8 at Amberley and Houghton, and 4 at Coldwaltham, that is 32 hides.

This charter was written in the year of our Lord's Incarnation 683, on the 3rd day of the month of August.

Lewes Martyrs

Sussex Protestants suffered grievously during the reign of Queen Mary. The ironmaster Richard Woodman, betrayed by his own brother, was one of 17 burned to death at Lewes. His testimony has survived.

A body of twelve men came towards evening and hid in the bushes near my house to watch for me, I being at home. One of my men and one of my children who came near them they detained, but my little girl suddenly saw them and ran indoors shouting 'Mother, mother, yonder cometh twenty men'. I was sitting on my bed and made to get out before they came, but my wife saw they were too near, and quickly closed the door, and barred it.

Now in my house was a hiding-place where I had lain time after time, even whilst the house was being searched, and this had happened I dare say twenty times. As soon as I had hid, my wife opened the door, and in answer to the men's questions declared I was not at home. 'Why did you shut the door, then?' She replied that she had been made afraid by the constant searching of the house, and feared injury to herself and the children.

Their search would have been once agin unavailing but my brother, who knew of my secret place, asked if they had searched there. It was a little loft over a window. They asked my wife the way into it, and she directed them into a chamber, and whilst they were searching called to me 'Away, away!' Knowing that now there was no remedy I wrenched some of the boards from the roof over my head but the noise drew the attention of my enemies. I got out, however, and leaped down, but had no shoes on. I ran down a lane that was full of sharp cinders, the men following me with swords drawn, shouting 'Strike him, strike him!' I was a good way ahead, but the words made me look back, and this in turn led to my capture, for I stepped upon a sharp cinder, and in endeavouring to save myself stumbled into a miry hole, and before I could rise a man known as Parker the Wild was on me, quickly followed by others. Had I had on my shoes I could have escaped, but it was not God's will.

Medieval Sussex Churches

For the dedicated and casual church visitor alike, a tour of medieval places of worship in Sussex can be a rewarding and enjoyable experience, even if the area does not immediately spring to mind when 'church' counties are discussed. There is no easily identfiable local style and most of the parish churches build before the middle of the sixteenth century are of modest size. The reasons for this are partly economic – Sussex in the later Middle Ages did not share in the prosperity enjoyed by East Anglia and the West Country which resulted in rebuilding of churches on a grandiose scale. Of the three largest churches only the diocesan cathedral of Chichster survives. The great Cluniac priory church of St Pancras at Lewes and the Benedictine abbey founded at Battle by William the Conqueror to commemorate his victory in 1066 were both destroyed during the Dissolution of the Monasteries under Henry VIII. The stylistic affiliations of all three lie outside Sussex and their architectural impact locally was on the whole peripheral. Some of the parish churches serving south coast ports, which date variously from the late Saxon period to the fifteenth century, were build on an impressive scale, and most of the other grander places of worship are former monastic churches and collegiate foundations like Boxgrove, Arundel and Etchingham. Sussex churches have also suffered from the heavy hands of Victorian restorers.

There are some unrestored gems, notably Burton, Didling and Warminghurst. Moreover, if the later medieval churches are few in number and relatively unimportant, the fact that after the early thirteenth century Sussex became a backwater in architectural terms has its positive side in the churches of the late eleventh to the early thirteenth centuries survive in considerable numbers. Most are simple and unpretentious, but many benefit from very attractive locations, notably some of the Downland churches which are often isolated from their scattered communities and have picturesque settings against the dramatic backcloth formed by the Downs. Didling and Coombes are good examples, the latter indistinguishable at a distance from a flint barn. Ford stands on its own in flat fields near the coast. Others like Greatham, Shermanbury, Wiston and Penhurst nestle close to the local great house, underlining the historically intimate relationship between parson and squire as patron of the living. The lasting impression of a typical Sussex church is of a modest structure dating principally from between the eleventh and early thirteenth centuries and comprising a square-ended chancel, unaisled nave, and lit by small round-headed or lancet windows, perhaps with a small timber porch, and a bell-tower capped by a shingled oak spire.

Richard Marks; Sussex Churches & Chapels *(1989)*

A Dialect ABC Psalm

The 19th century fascination with the Sussex dialect which led Rev William Parish to compile his famous dictionary also produced at least two versions of Biblical texts. Mark Anthony Lower, a prolific Sussex author and a founder of the Sussex Archaeological Society, wrote a Sussex dialect version of 'The Song of Solomon', while James Richards (under the pseudonym Jim Cladpole) turned his pen to the Acrostic Psalms – those in which the initial letters of certain verses and/or lines spell out the Hebrew alphabet. The Younsmere Press brought out a selection in 1992.

Psalm 37

Acos of evildoers doant you git into a stew;
    And doant you be green against de workers in sin.
    For dey shall soon be mowed down like grass,
    And shrivel up like green yarbs.
Bank on de LORD, and do good;
    Settle in de land, and taak faithfulness to your bosom.
    So will you be happy in de LORD;
    And He will give you what your heart wishes for.
Cast your lot into de lap of de LORD;

Bank also on Him, and He will bring it off alright.
And He will maak your rightdoing come out as de light,
And what be your right as clear as noonday.
Deed yourself to de LORD, and bide He's time;
Doant git into a stew acros of him who gits on in he's own
way,
Acos of de man who gits on by wicked plans.
End up being angry, and forsake wrath;
Doant git into a stew, it onny leads to evildoing.
For evildoers shall be cut off;
But hem who wait for de LORD, dey shall inherit de land.

Jim Cladpole (JamesRichards); De A.B.C. Psalms Put into de Sussex dialect and
in due A.B.C. feshion *(1938)*

Rustics at Worship

Thomas Geering was born in Hailsham in 1813 and never moved
away. His memoirs, originally entitled Our Parish: A Medley *were*
first republished under their present title in 1925 after falling out of
print and being 'discovered' by Arthur Beckett.

It was a pleasing sight in years gone by to see the rustics of the parish
assemble on a Sunday afternoon and hang about the church door ere
they entered and take up their seats, all dressed in the smock-frock
and hobnailed boots, and with hair cut straight across the forehead
and all round as though a basin had been clapped on the head as a
guide to the scissors of the homespun barber; and I well remember
these same youths passing the reading-desk, with chin almost resting
on the breast, 'demure and grave', many of them dropping the curate
a reverential bow as they followed each one on to his appointed place.
Behaviour since that time has somewhat changed, but reverence, if not
so demonstrable, may be deeper. One thing is certain; the smock-frock
and the hobnails are never now seen or heard within the portals of the
church door. Fashion, following close upon the heels of progress and
means, has banished the rustic garb. For dress 'tis hard now to know
the maid from the mistress and the manservant from the master.
If veneration for the ritual is changing or passing away, there is no

change in veneration for the buiding or for God's Acre. All this is sacred and hallowed. We may forget some living acquaintance, but here are friends we shall never forget. As I pass daily among the graves some occupants of the cold and lone home rises and stands before me – not shrouded nor ghostly, nor wan, nor weary. I see them, and hold converse with them as of old. We will walk the paths together, but talk on no new subject. Their present is my future. We touch not that mystery. It is some episode of the past that engages our thoughts and tongues for a few seconds: it may be the glimpse of a beloved child who has risen and is standing before me, or sister, brother, or parent who is awakening and tightening the cords of broken and almost forgotten love; it may be a mother's or a wife's caress, or it may be a father's rebuke. And so we people our brains with associations of the past. The reverie is salutary, and our loved ones retire to their cerements.

Thomas Geering; Our Sussex Parish *(1884)*

The Cathedral Spire

The story of the cathedral can start almost anywhere in south-west Sussex. Chichester from the Selsey peninsula is like Charters from the Beauce: no other English cathedral, not even Lincoln, exerts such a continuous presence on the flat surrounding countryside, and it is the continuity which is the important thing; the spire becomes as invariable and natural as the sky and sun. What Chichester has in addition, on any kind of clear day – and there are a lot of clear days in Sussex – is the gently rising backcloth of the South Downs two or three miles away, so that God, man and nature always seem to be in equilibrium. And from anywhere on those slopes, behind Goodwood or on Bow Hill, the effect is unforgettable: the plain like a sea, tipped with a glitter or a shimmer which really is the sea, punctuated only by one slim spire. Nothing of the same height must ever be built near Chichester: spire and countryside form an equation or a symbol experienced by millions of people every year, which cannot be given a value purely in terms of landscape or architecture.

Ian Nairn; The Buildings of England: Sussex *(1965)*

Turmoil at the Altar

John Coker Egerton's distinctive style and sense of humour in suggested by the subtitle he gave his Sussex Folk *and* Sussex Ways: *'Stray Studies in the Wealden Formation of Human Nature'. The rector of Burwash from 1867, he revelled in human diversity. The 'asking' in this extract refers to the reading of the banns.*

The marriage service itself used to be far more productive of scenes than it is now, and education is doing much to secure outward decorum, at any rate during the ceremony. Occasionally, however, still one's nerves are sorely taxed by things said and done under the combined influence of nervousness, ignorance and shyness. I did not argue much good from the preliminary questions of a 'hopper' who stopped me in the village street on Saturday evening after dark, and said 'Please, sir, can you ask me twice one Sunday?' – meaning, I suppose, at morning and afternoon service both.

'No, friend,' I replied. 'I can't do that.'

Then, after a pause: 'Please, sir, can you marry me the same Sunday I'm asked out?' was his next enquiry.

I was obliged, of course, to say that I would not accommodate him even in this way.

'But,' I added, 'what makes you in such a hurry?'

'Well, you see, sir,' he said, 'we're hoppers, and we don't want to be stopping about here after hops are done.'

I agreed to marry them at eight o'clock on the Monday morning after they were 'out-asked', and they accordingly presented themselves. All went well for a time, till suddenly the bridegroom put his head between his hands, began to cry, and walked away to the other end of the church. The bride did not look as much surprised as I should have expected, and the groomsman, another huge 'hopper', seemed barely surprised at all. Seeing, however, that his mate showed no signs of coming back, he turned half round and called out with a loud voice: 'Come, Joe, be a man; stand up like a man, Joe.'

Upon this Joe slowly returned and stood up and said what was necessary. He went away again, but not till the essential part of the service was finished. After the service I asked the clerk what the meaning of this behaviour was. I thought it must have been that the man was worse for drink, but the explanation was that he had not long buried his first wife, and that he was overcome by his feelings.

A friend of mine in the next parish but one told me some years ago of a wedding experience which happened to him, and in which I sincerely hope that he kept his countenance. The couple being married was a specially rustic one; it was the winter-time and the bridegroom had a bad cold; he had managed with a sad snuffle to say the words in a fashion after the clergyman till the betrothal; but then, having both hands occupied in holding the ring on the bride's finger, and fearing probably that if he let go he should invalidate the ceremony, he felt the coming difficulty, and so, while waiting to be 'taught by the priest', instead of beginning 'With this ring I thee wed,' he turned round to his groomsman, and said, in the most matter-of-fact voice: 'Wipe my noase for me, will 'ee, Bill?'

John Coker Egerton; Sussex Folk and Sussex Ways (1884)

From the Parish Records

Ashburnham, 1576
Buried Thomas Winfield, that old fornicator.

Salehurst, 1610
Henry Turner, a profane drunkard, died excommunicate and was buried in ye highway to the terror of all drunkards.

Buxted, 1666
Richard Bassett, the old Clerk of this parish who had continued in the offices of Clerk & Sexton in this Parish by the space of 43 years, whose melody warbled forth as if he had been thumped in the back with a stone, was buried the 20th day of September.

Wadhurst, 1691
Baptised Elizabeth, daughter of Francis and Ann Comber. This child was heard crying in the womb before it was born.

Angmering, 1757
Baptised James, son of Widow Crossingham, sworn & confessed to

have been begotten by her late husband's son. Upon examining the
lad, he solemnly declared the hussy attacked him on his bed, first in
her clothes, then naked. He did not comply. But afterwards she
rushed into his bed naked & seized the premises.

Angmering, 1765
Baptised William, son of Anne Robarts by God Knows Who.

Fletching, 1767
Buried Pleasante Sharpe, the concubine of the late Thomas Hall, by whom
she had 4 natural children. Pretended to be his wife till a discovery was
made by his real wife coming here the very day one of the children was
baptised. They both did a public penance for their iniquities.

Rotherfield, 1768
Buried a travelling man, a viper catcher.

Wadhurst, 1784
Baptised Harriet, base born daughter of Elizabeth Rogers, a very
noted Strumpet of this Parish.

St Clement's, Hastings, 1817
Buried Richard Harlot, 63, a razor grinder – cut his own throat.

Fishers of Men at Hastings

It was the moral rather than the physical health of the fishing
community that began to worry middle class reformers in the late
1840s. There is no record of the fishermen actually asking for any
assistance with their morals, but nonetheless a movement arose in the
early 1850s focusing on the need to come to their aid. In June, 1848,
a Sunday school superintendent summed up the reformers' concerns.
He said he was particularly worried about the small child, 'taught by
example, as he is, to think it childish to go to school, to church or to
chapel, and manly to help "father" on Sunday at the boat, and, with
his hands thrust into his pockets, to swagger along trying his skill at
smoking and swearing'.

A teacher said in 1852 he thought the fisher lads lived in 'a state of great mental darkness'. As there were schools to improve the young already in existence in the Old Town at that time, the main concern of the reformers was to turn the fishermen away from alcohol and the 'evils' that were considered to accompany it.

The well-known Old Town scripture reader Tom Tanner was ordained a deacon by the bishop of Chichester in March, 1853, and set about 'promoting the spiritual good of the fishermen'. The Hastings fishermen have often been seen as being in some way different from their neighbours, and in the mid-19th century they were frequently described as a 'tribe', a 'race' or even as 'aborigines'. Adopting the appropriate missionary spirit, the Reverend Tom Tanner was sent to Rock-a-Nore to tackle the heathens on their own ground. Within a few months the church authorities announced that a 'Fishermen's Church' was to be built there, at a cost of £529. The foundation stone of the building, now the Fishermen's Museum in Rock-a-Nore, was laid in August, 1853. Unfortunately no notable person could be found to carry out the stone-laying ceremony, and the historic deed had to be performed by the Deputy Pierwarden. 'This apathy does not augur well,' commented the *Hastings Chronicle*.

Steve Peak; Fishermen of Hastings *(1985)*

Divine Mercy

Whereas ffrancis Selwyn, esq., and Mrs Penelope Selwyn and Mrs Susan Pell are very aged and to my knowledge very sickely and that Mrs Mary Selwyn daughter of the said ffrancis is at the present very sicke and soe hath been for many months together therefore by verture of an act of parliament authorising me so to doe give lisence to the same persons above mentioned to eat flesh dyet in Lent and upon other fish Dayes as the Law does allow. Witnes my hand ye 5 of march 1660. Will. Wallace.

From the Friston parish register, March 5, 1660

Anti-Catholic Feeling in Lewes

There are no November 5th celebrations anywhere in England to compare with those at Lewes. Today the atmosphere is good-natured, if boisterous, but during the 19th century the event was marred by religious bigotry.

It was at the firesite that the Bonfire Boys expressed their religious and political allegiances. While 'No Popery' banners were carried in the processions it was through the speeches of the mock clerics, the effigies and the tableaux that the Bonfire Boys' anti-Catholicism was expressed. Resplendent in such grandiose titles as Bishop of Newtown, The Lord Bishop of the Cliffe or His Grace the Archbishop of St John-sub-Castro, the mock clerics became the official mouthpiece of their societies. It was their appointed task to harangue the crowd before condemning the effigies to the fire. Through the nineteenth century their speeches took on a strong anti-Catholic tone, the Papacy continuing to be perceived as a threat to Protestant Britain. In a typical firesite speech in 1874 the Bishop of Cliffe forcefully expressed the opinion that 'what the Catholics aspire to is universal dominion all over the world, with the Pope at their head'. He continued, 'We must remember that they are now what they always were in ancient times, and had they the power they would put an end to Protestantism.'

Such attitudes were given symbolic representation by the annual burning of the effigy of the Pope in the company of the conspirator Guy Fawkes. In 1851 the effigies of the Pope and [Cardinal] Wiseman were paraded around the town before being burnt on the fire outside county Hall, but in the following year the Pope suffered this fate alone. In the period leading up to 1913 the effigies of Pius IX, whose pontificate lasted from 1846 to 1878, and that of his successor Leo XIII were burnt. The Bonfire Boys were frequently criticised by Catholics and more tolerant Protestants for this expression of religious bigotry, and such was the controvery aroused by Pope-burning that the matter was raised in the House of Commons in 1902 by Mr J. Tully, member for South Leitrim, when he asked the Secretary of State for the Home Department whether he was aware of the occurrences in Lewes. Either in response to such criticism or because of a change in attitude, the Commercial Square in 1893 burnt an effigy of Pope Paul V, the Pope at the time of the Gunpowder Plot. However, the other societies continued to burn the offending effigy of the incumbent Pope.

Jim Etherington; Lewes Bonfire Night *(1993)*

No Popery Today

Cliffe takes the business of marching seriously and the proliferation of torch-bearing warriors in the shape of Vikings, Cavaliers and Roundheads intensifies the grimmer but captivating atmosphere. Banners carried beneath those already stretched across the narrow street remember the Lewes martyrs, the discovery of the Gunpowder Plot and the arrival on our shores of the one-time saviour of English Protestant rule, William of Orange, on another November 5th in 1688. In this commemoration one can see more clearly the link some draw between Lewes Bonfire and the 'marching season' in parts of Northern Ireland. What connections remain are largely of historical value rather than contemporary, although the Reverend Ian Paisley – to the societies' disapproval – did once turn up to witness the proceedings and has preached in the town at the old Jireh chapel, where a Bonfire service, somewhat controversially, is still held each year.

Guy Fawkes, of course, and a snarling figure of Pope Paul V are carried to their doom, chaperoned by the inevitable blazing letters no popery. Other effigies sof more local significance usually bob by; the Enemies of Bonfire, large firework-packed papier-maché severed heads on pikes portraying authority or community figures who may have crossed the Society in the last twelve months. Councillors, MPs, even priests, have all found their images raised and bleeding above the crowds on the Fifth. This year banner-squabbling Bonfire Boys themselves are targeted. No-one is too sacred to be an Enemy.

But here is what many have come to see, its upper portion peering over the hump of Cliffe Bridge before dramatically swinging into full view. A huge, brilliantly executed and lavishly painted pyrotechnic sculpture, dragged on wheels by sweating Bonfire Boys and Girls, looms high over the crowds through which laughter and applause ripple. This year America's President Clinton and his clandestine physical pleasures are lampooned in an obscene tribute of phallic Cruise missiles, Viagra, Bill as Captain America and hilarious slogans unfit to print. Past works of art still linger in the memory . . . the BSE crisis, John Major . . . you can guess many of them but there's always a twist of genius and humour in the execution and this year is no exception. Again, Lewes shows its righteous anger at those who abuse positions of power for their own ends. It almost seems a shame to explode these marvels, but explode they must to drive their point home.

Andy Thomas; Streets of Fire *(1999)*

The Market Cross at Chichester

For any visitor to Chichester, as to the residents of the city, the Cross is a powerful image: from far along East Street, South Street and West Street this seemingly quaint and antique structure, Chichester Market Cross, draws one forward. Arriving within its orbit, however, one is immediately faced with the puzzle of how best to engage with it. From the crowds that regularly circle it, the Cross is evidently a focal point, but one that is 'unattended', for everyone seems busily occupied about some business *other than that of its history or beauty*, for they live its purpose . . . and use it as a meeting place, a crossroads.

But turn one's attention to the Cross itself and one finds it invites one to walk round it, even to walk into it: although any thought of walking *through* it must be quickly abandoned for this is neither a building that can be ignored nor one to be briskly shouldered aside in a gesture of modernist hauteur. Glancing up, on the north side, one is startled to see two wide-mouthed gargoyles (are they *human* faces?), and then drawn ineluctably round the entire structure to marvel at the inverted winged-monster, the sea-horse and the goat (on the north-east face); the double-headed eagle and the stallion (on the south-east face); the sheep and salmon (on the south face); and the deer, the wyvern, the camel and a winged lion – all on the south-west face. But then, moving inside, and sitting on the stone bench that circles the central pillar (it has a girth – I trailed a piece of string all round and measured it – of just over twelve and a half feet), one glances up to the vault to find several bosses of foliage and fruit – and gradually senses the whole structure begins to speak not as some odd curiosity but as a building with a continued and vital purpose.

As we know, the Cross dates from 1501, but the fact that it has no obvious 'front' or 'back' aligns it immediately with the finest of modern sculpture, a piece, say, such as Rodin's *The Kiss*, which invites similar attention for, although it was first cast in 1882, it also has no obvious viewpoint. Sited as the Cross is, at the very centre of the city, and not only of the city but, symbolically, at the centre of local and county administration (of Chichester District Council and of West Sussex County Council – whose administrative offices are both located within the city), the Cross provides an easily recognised but also evocative 'heart' to the three authorities – city, district and county. But that 'heart' is not restricted to a secular role, for the Cross is intimately related to a spiritual centre, the cathedral (and many prints and photographs deliberately show both buildings in the single image) and, as we know, was gifted to citizens by Edward Story, bishop of the diocese of Chichester.

Paul Foster; 'Let the Cross Speak' from A Jewel in Stone *(2001)*

5 · THE VILLAGES

This is where the anthologist inevitably brings the wrath of the partisan upon his head. We all have our favourite villages, and in 'privileging' Ditchling, Amberley, Alfriston and Lindfield I have cravenly played the populist card: these are among the acknowledged gems, whatever your own preference may be. We begin with some which have disappeared, as featured in a magazine which has, alas, also vanished, despite its popularity among readers who saw it as a successor of the old Sussex County Magazine. *John Vigar's article was in due course followed by a book,* Lost Villages of Sussex.

Humps and Bumps

In an age when the countryside is under constant threat from ever-inceasing urban expansion, it may seem strange to reflect on the disappearance of homes from the same area over the past 600 years.

When agriculture formed the basis of everyone's lives, there were few large areas of absolutely undeveloped countryside. Instead, small settlements grew up where the geology of the land matched itself to the requirements of either arable farming or animal husbandry.

Of course the majority of these early settlements – most of which were in place by the time of the Domesday Book was compiled in 1086 – have since grown into the towns and villages in which we spend most of our lives. Yet here and there settlements have been destroyed, abandoned or moved to suit the requirements of a new generation. Sometimes nothing remains above ground – although there is usually some reminder in the form of an isolated church, a farm or a dead-end road, to indicate the former settlements.

There are many reasons why settlements became unsatisfactory, but the best known is undoubtedly the Black Death. This plague, which crossed Sussex in 1348 and 1349, resulted in a reduction in population of up to 45 per cent. Isolated farming settlements, made up of just a few families, were badly hit, and no longer had the manpower to cultivate sufficient food for their survival – so they abandoned the traditional farmstead and teamed up with other people in a similar predicament.

At Bargham, near Angmering, five miles from Worthing, are the scanty remains of a church whose last rector was installed in 1521. For more than 600 years this church served a small farming community, settled in a fertile valley. Following the Black Death, the community was forced to change its agricultural practices, resulting in the almost total loss of the entire settlement.

There was a general move away from the labour intensive arable farming and towards animal husbandry. This required fewer workers, allowing many to move to towns or take up some other trade or craft that required easy access to raw materials or a ready market. This great move of population can be studied throughout Sussex.

Another significant cause of de-population occurred when any lord of the manor decided to empark his house, or to landscape his grounds. Villages which had often been established for centuries were demolished and replaced by new houses on the edge of the estate – or at least out of the way. While this technique could easily be applied to houses, most – but not all – lords of the manor could not bring themselves to demolish the parish church, which often stands as sole survivor of a once-bustling settlement.

The best example in Sussex is at Parham, where the little church stands isolated in the park of the big house, having lost its village by forceable means in the late 18th century.

John Vigar; Downs Country Magazine, *Autumn (1994)*

Villages of the Downs and the Weald

I have no particular village in mind. Sussex has a series which conforms to a type though with many variations. The villages of the Downs are not like those of the Weald. They are, taken generally, smaller; the houses cluster close together for company, forming an oasis in a lovely desert, and the church, nearly always of pre-Norman beginning, dominates the view like a mother with her children. I have in my mind at the moment West Dean Orientalis, secluded, compact, and the the understanding eye can read the whole history of the hamlet in its general features, place-names, and the monuments in the church. There is Telscombe in a saucer-like hollow, not as it is now with sprawling new outgrowths, but as I saw it twenty years ago when it was as it had been for centuries – the home of ploughman, shepherd and yeoman farmer; a tiny church and a tiny school; and a life moving very much as it had in Stuart and Tudor times.

The Wealden villages of Sussex are not usually so compact. The woodlands which form the principal feature have drawn to them a resident gentry. That is especially so since the industrial revolution of the nineteenth century. It is surprising how many of the ironmasters of the north dwell in Sussex and on the Surrey confines. Merchant princes in the buying, selling and distributive trades of London are scattered about. These, with the landed gentry of an older time, give a touch to the Wealden village which is absent on the downs. Here are, speaking generally, bigger churches and fine timbered cottages, homes of literary celebrities and middle-class people. The countryfolk are not entirely agricultural, but predominantly gardeners, a highly intelligent class of worker. The gamekeeper, I would like to love him, for he has the odour of deep woods and wild places about him, but that he is so destructive of all things except the sacred pheasants and partridges. Villages like Lindfield, Mayfield, or small ones like Heyshott in the West and Northiam in the east have an opulent beauty widely different from that of downland hamlets.

A.A. Evans; On Foot in Sussex (1933)

Ditchling

Ditchling is a village set almost in the centre of Sussex – it is almost in line with Chailey Common, whose white and toy-like windmill and pointed trees are generally considered to mark the middle of Sussex. There are people who hold it the best village in Sussex, not because it is the most beautiful, or the most unspoiled, for unfortunately its popularity has resulted in some undesirable buildings on its edges. But it is superbly set in regard to the Downs on a little hill of sandrock, at the perfect distance away to survey the chalk range as whole from Black Cap to Chanctonbury and beyond. The string of little old villages close under the Downs, such as Fulking and Edburton and Clayton, are much too close to see the Downs as anything but an overshadowing presence. But Ditchling is just far enough away to gain a wide-spreading impression of their lovely sweeping line, and yet so near that a twenty minutes' walk brings any inhabitant to the foot of the hill.

The central point of the little eminence on which Ditchling is built is crowned by a very beautiful and very Sussex-looking church. If St Margaret's church was snatched up by a giant hand and set down in Warwickshire or Somerset – county of stately Perpendicular towers – it would cry 'Sussex' so loudly that it would have to be put back again without any delay. It is built of flint – the most Sussex of all building materials, some of the work knapped and fine, some coarser and of whole flints. It has a low tower with a pointed cap covered with oak shingles. There is an idea, from the strength of the masonry of the supporting arches, that the central tower – it is a cruciform church – was intended to be considerably higher than it actually is, but few Ditchling people would desire it raised by even a foot – the nave and chancel, the north and south aisles, with the low central tower, give a motherly and brooding look to the church which a higher tower would spoil.

In the churchyard, which from its elevation yields most delightful views both of the red roofs of the village and of the Downs, there are, among the more permanent and usual stone and marble tombstones, one or two of those rapidly decaying long low wooden grave-boards which recall old wood-engravings illustrating Gray's 'Elegy in a Country Churchyard' – the most essentially English of all English poems. One of these grave-boards is to the memory of George Howell, who was born at West Hoathly on 6 June 1754 and who died at Ditchling on 7 May 1855, aged, so the inscription proudly states, 100 years and 336 days. What the span of such a life had covered – when he was born the French Revolution and the Napoleonic Wars were in the future, the name of Nelson was unkown to English history and Trafalgar and Waterloo unfought. Railways did not exist, and not one of Dickens' novels was written. When he died the last of the Hanoverian Georges was dead and Queen Victoria was seated on that throne which she occupied for so long. And it is tolerably safe to say that through all those events George Howell probably spent the whole of his long life within the confines of Sussex – a visit to Brighthelmstone being possibly the furthest extent of his travels between the seculded and charming village of his birth and Ditchling, where he died, and where his bones have rested for nearly another hundred years.

Esther Meynell; Sussex (1947)

Felpham

William Blake lived at Felpham for about three years, at the invitation of the poet William Hayley (the 'bless'd hermit' of the verse). His stay was not without incident (see page 116) but he came to love the village, which he called 'the sweetest spot on earth'. These lines, with their typical Blakeian religious imagery, were written for his friend Mrs Anna Flaxman.

This song to the flower of Flaxman's joy;
To the blossom of hope, for a sweet decoy;
Do all that you can, or all that you may,
To entice him to Felpham and far away.

Away to sweet Felpham, for Heaven is there;
The Ladder of Angels descends through the air;
On the turret its spiral does softly descend,
Through the village then winds, at my cot it does end.

You stand in the village and look up to Heaven;
The precious stones glitter on flights seventy-seven;
And my brother is there, and my friends and thine
Descend and ascend with the bread and the wine.

The bread of sweet thoughts and the wine of delight
Feed the village of Felpham by day and by night,
And at his own door the bless'd hermit does stand
Dispensing unceasing to all the wide land.

Amberley God Knows

Amberley needs no defence, but having recently written a history of the castle, I should perhaps point that it is now a highly successful and atmospheric country house hotel rather than a ruin.

'Amberley God knows' is a name almost as common in the rural mouth of Sussex as Botley 'Assizes' in the vulgar tongue of Hampshire; and Amberley folk are also credited with being web-footed. Both title and assertion have their origin in the situation of the village, which stretches along a low escarpment of chalk into the marshes of the Arun at the foot of the most solitary portion of our Downs. It lies off the main roads, and until our Sussex artists 'discovered' it, was probably as little known and visited as any place of human habitation could well be. This would seem to point to the derivation of its somewhat irreverent cognomen.

There is the variant of the phrase, which Mr Lucas point out – 'In winter, if you ask an Amberley man where he dwells, he says "Amberley, God help us". In summer he says, "Amberley, where *would* you live?"' 'Amberley, God knows' is, however, the name it is known by and called of Sussex country folk.

The village itself bears witness to its secluded isolation. Most of the houses are thatched and old enough to satisfy the Knights of the Brush, to whom ramshackledom and 'local colour' are so dear. That which the housewife calls mildew and dust, the artist blesses and reproduces with his choicest tints. A long street ends at the church, beyond which lies the castle, whose history is akin to itself in unheroic, humdrum simplicity.

Romance has endeavoured to plume itself within its walls, but with little result. Whether it ever echoed to war's alarms and shocks is very doubtful. A country residence of the Bishops of Chichester originally, it was 'embattled' in medieval times by Bishop Reed. Bishop Sherborne, in the sixteenth century, built the dwelling-house inside the walls. There are 'donjons' and cells below the entrance, which is flanked by two round towers. The whole is an oblong of massive walls, and from the marsh to the north forms a fine view notwithstanding that there are few points raised above the ruined parapet. The chapel, inside, has a large beech tree growing in its midst, and the whole of the enclosure is a beautiful lawn bordered by young trees.

Arthur Stanley Cooke; Off the Beaten Track in Sussex

Greatham

For peace, than knowledge more desirable,
    Into your Sussex quietness I came,
When summer's green and gold and azure fell
    Over the world in flame.

And peace upon your pasture-lands I found,
    When grazing flocks drift on continually,
As little clouds that travel with no sound
    Across a windless sky.

Out of your oaks the birds call to their mates
    That brood among the pines, where hidden deep
From curious eyes a world's adventure waits
    In columned choirs of sleep.

Under the calm ascensions of the night
    We heard the mellow lapsing and return
Of night-owls purring in their groundling flight
    Through lanes of darkling fern.

Unbroken peace when all the stars were drawn
    Back to their lairs of light, and ranked along
From shire to shire the downs out of the dawn
    Were risen in golden song.

John Drinkwater; 'Of Greatham'

Alfriston

A short mile further and we recross the Cuckmere by a footbridge and reach Alfriston, a very prettily situated village, full of interesting objects. We are now at the entrance of the gap by which the Cuckmere breaks through the main line of the Downs, and, as in the cases of the similar gaps formed by the Ouse and the Adur, all the beauty of the valley is concentrated at this point. But the beauty of the village is quite independent of the river, and is best seen from the downs, which rise from it on both sides. When viewed from above, the way in which the red-tiled houses interspersed with trees and gardens, group themselves round the old church tower is very fascinating. A little to the north, on the eastern bank of the river, can be traced the site of Burghlow Castle, clearly built to defend the Cuckmere.

The grand cruciform church is of a large size for a Sussex village, and is sometimes called the Cathedral of the Downs. The legend of its foundation is of a kind quite typical of East Sussex. The original intention of the founder was to build it on another site, but night after night the stones and timber were miraculously conveyed to the Tye, the piece of common land where it now stands. Presently a wise man, noticing four oxen lying in the Tye in the form of a cross, advised that the church should be built there and that it should be cruciform in shape.

Just south of the Tye, and close to the church, with which it is coeval, is the interesting ancient parsonage – a fine timber-built house with a thatched roof – which was purchased by the National Trust in 1898. The old hall shows some interior timberwork. Another picturesque building is the old Star Inn, in date not much later than 1500, with very singular carving on the outside, including representations of St George and the dragon and St Giles with his hind. The old lion at the corner is said to be the figure-head of a Dutch ship wrecked in Cuckmere Haven. At the end of the street are the mutilated remains of a village cross, crowned with a later stone which looks like a hat. In many counties these crosses are common enough, but this is the only one in Sussex, excepting the beautiful market cross at Chichester.

F.G. *Brabant;* Rambles in Sussex *(1909)*

Lindfield

Lindfield, immediately north-east of Haywards Heath, has long been regarded as one of the most picturesque of Sussex villages, a status confirmed in 1934 when it was so voted by readers of the *Sussex County Magazine*. Lindfield possesses what Pevsner declares to be 'without any doubt the finest village street in East Sussex', a half mile-long collection of houses and cottages, with the thirteenth century church of St John the Baptist at one end and the pond and the extensive green at the other. It is, in short, what many people would regard as the typical English village and consequently receives many visitors.

Lindfield was not always so pleasant a place, and in the years immediately after the Napoleonic Wars many of its inhabitants, like so many in Sussex, lived in great poverty. In 1824 the Quaker William Allen settled at Gravelye House in Lindfield, and on 100 acres on the south side of West Common, bought by his friend John Smith MP, of Dale Park, he set up a number of smallholdings. These, complete with cottage and stock, he let out at a rent of 4s per week. After a hesitant start the scheme became a great success and Allen went on to build a school, teaching workshop, a boarding school for poor children from Ireland and elsewhere, and a library. He and his wife taught some of the local people to read, and a newspaper was produced. Allen's work attracted great attention and he worked tirelessly to improve the lot of the underprivileged far beyond Lindfield and Sussex. He was an associate of Wilberforce in his campaign to abolish slavery, a partner of Robert Owen, the great socialist, and also a friend of the Duke of Sussex and the Czar of Russia. He twice visited Russia, setting up settlements there, founded twenty schools in Greence and worked for reform in Spain. This extraordinary man died in Lindfield in 1843, leaving the village vastly more prosperous than he had found it.

Michael H.C. Baker; Sussex Villages (1977)

6 . ON THE ROAD

Those of us who live in Sussex must learn to love our roads for what they are – meandering reminders of the early days of travel. Getting about from west to east is certainly a slow business, even on stretches of the A27. It was harder still in days gone by, even though the Romans had set a good example.

Stane Street

This road is by far the best known in the whole Wealden area, indeed it is the only one which appears, over most of its length, to have been recognised as a Roman road since early times, and its main alignments still remain a very striking feature on the modern map of West Sussex.

The road connects Chichester – *Noviomagus*, the tribal capital of Roman Sussex – with London by the most direct route that the lie of the land allows; it is an extremely good example of the skill and thoroughness with which these roads were planned by the Roman engineers to secure the shortest route with the greatest avoidance of natural obstacles . . .

Quite a number of inhabited sites are known along this road. First of all, there were the *mansiones* or posting stations. Two of these, at Hardham and Alfoldean, are still traceable and their remains have been examined. They were small rectangular enclosures, through which the road ran centrally, containing buildings that were required to deal with the needs of traffic, just as did the coaching inns in later

times. A posting system for officials and other travellers existed on all
important routes in the Roman Empire, and their undoubted presence
here indicates that Stane Street was an important highway.

Besides these stations and their attendant outskirts, there was the
large villa at Bignor, well known for its fine mosaic floors, which was
in existence probably well before AD100 and a number of lesser-
known villas and farms in the neighbourhood of Pulborough, also of
early date.

Ivan D. Margary; Roman Ways in the Weald (1948)

An Overturned Coach

Sussex roads were terrible until comparatively recent times. An old
rhyme credits 'Sowseks' with 'dirt and myre', and Dr Burton, the
author of the Iter Sussexiensis, humorously found it a reason why
Sussex people and beasts had such long legs.

'Come now, my friend,' he wrote, in Greek, 'I will set before you a
sort of problem in Aristotle's fashion: Why is it that the oxen, the
swine, the women, and all other animals, are so long legged in Sussex?
May it be from the difficulty of pulling the feet out of so much mud
by the strength of the ankle, that the muscles get stretched, as it were,
and the bones lengthened?'

When, in 1703, the King of Spain visited the Duke of Somerset at
Petworth, he had the greatest difficulty in getting here. One of his
attendants has put on record the perils of the journey: 'We set out a six
o'clock in the morning (at Portsmouth) to go to Petworth, and did not
get out of the coaches, save only when we overturned or stuck fast in
the mire, till we arrived at our journey's end. 'Twas hard service for the
prince to sit fourteen hours in the coach that day, without eating
anything and passing through the worst ways that I ever saw in my life:
we were thrown but once indeed in going, but both our coach which
was leading and his highness's body coach would have suffered very
often if the nimble boors of Sussex had not frequently poised it, or
supported it with their shoulders, from Godalming to Petworth; and
the nearer we approached the duke's, the more inaccessible it seemed
to be. The last nine miles of the way cost six hours time to conquer.'

E.V. Lucas; Highways and Byways in Sussex (1907)

Pulled by Oxen

I came to Lewes from Tunbridge through the deepest, dirtiest, but many ways the richest and most profitable country in all that part of England. The timber I saw there was prodigious, as well in quality as bigness, and in some places to be suffered to grow only because it was so far off any navigation that it was not worth cutting down and carrying away. In dry summers, indeed, a great deal is carried away to Maidstone, and sometimes I have seen one tree on a carriage drawn by two and twenty oxen, and even then it is carried so little a way, that it is sometimes two or three years before it gets to Chatham; for if once the rains come on it stirs no more that year, and sometimes a whole summer is not enough to make the roads passable. Here I had a sight which indeed I never saw in any other part of Egland, viz. the going to church at a country village not far from Lewes. I saw an antient lady of very good family, I assure you, drawn to church in her coach by six oxen; nor was this done in frolick or humour, but mere necessity, the way being so stiff and deep that no horses could go in it.

Daniel Defoe; A Tour Thro' the Whole Island of Great Britain *(1724)*

An Early Coach Service

This is the first record of a service between Sussex and the capital. By June 1811, with the sea-water cure in full spate, there were no fewer than 28 coaches running between Brighton and London.

Thomas Smith, the old Lewes carrier, being dead, the business is now continued by his widow, Mary Smith, who gets into the 'George Inn' in the Borough, Southwark, every Wednesday in the afternoon, and sets out for Lewes every Thursday morning by eight o'clock, and brings Goods and Passengers to Lewes, Fletching, Chayley, Newick and all places adjacent at reasonable rates.

Performed (if God permit) by Mary Smith.

Advertisement in The Lewes Journal, *December 8, 1746*

Slowly Does It

Nathaniel Blaker became an eminent surgeon, but his memoirs were largely devoted to his early life in the Fulking area: his parents moved to Perching Manor Farm in Edburton before his first birthday.

It would be difficult, or almost impossible, for people living in the early part of the twentieth century, and accustomed to the luxurious and rapid travelling, with all the means and appliances for comfort of the present day, to realise that in the forties and even the fifties of the nineteenth century the ordinary rate of travelling was only from about six to ten, or at most, twelve miles an hour: that the roads, except the large thoroughfares along which coaches frequently ran, were so narrow that vehicles could only pass with considerable care, that they were mended with flints coarsely broken, if broken at all, and that these were put on in the autumn, and were ground in by the wheels of carts and other vehicles during the next winter, and that, if put on too late, or if the winter happened to be unusually dry, they remained loose all the next summer. Horses with broken knees were very common objects and the jolting of the vehicles, even with the best springs, was very tiring; a journey of any considerable distance was a matter of some importance, and preparations were made days beforehand.

There was a common saying: 'A man must go to London once or else he will die a fool', and going to London was looked on as a great event. My father used to relate that he started on his first visit to London from Selmeston, close to Berwick Station, with his father very early in the morning on horseback, dressed in a new suit of clothes and new top-boots. I can well recollect Queen Victoria coming from London to Brighton by road, and seeing her in her carriage with her escort round her pass through Pyecombe; and I also recollect the coaches with their teams of splendid horses running between London and Brighton, and presenting a most imposing appearance especially at night when their approach was announced by the bugle and they were lighted up with a number of lamps, and seeming to bear down upon you like a big ball of fire. Horses on the road were frequently frightened by them and I well remember, when I was taken to Pyecombe to see my relations, being kept awake till 10pm or later, because my father was afraid to start on his road home till the last coach had passed.

N.P. *Blaker; Sussex in Bygone Days (1919)*

Turnpikes in the Cuckmere Valley

The trackways of Sussex were in a deplorable condition by the 18th century, having been used extensively for droving and for the heavy, broad-wheeled Sussex wagons drawn by teams of oxen, as well as for transporting iron goods, although Acts of Parliament had obliged ironmasters to deposit specified amounts of stone and metalling on surfaces of roads they used. The age of the turnpike road arrived, and, although unpopular, they were certainly necessary if transportation was to improve. Some bridges became necessary as new turnpike roads crossed the river. These roads were maintained by payments by users at the turnpike gates set up along the routes. Some modern roads in the Cuckmere valley follow turnpike routes, at least in parts, and other turnpike roads exist as trackways which are still traceable. The principal routes fording the lower Cuckmere had been created centuries earlier, and some early turnpikes approximated to these older routes. The old trackway which ran from Lewes to Eastbourne via Longbridge was turnpiked in 1759. It ran from Southerham, along the Ranscombe coaching road over the salt flats at Glynde, and into Glynde village, across Glynde Reach, and on or around the back of Firle Park. The road was an old Downland bostal as far as Bopeep, Alciston, when it descended and ran along the trackway which is still today a beautiful underhill walk, past New Barn, Berwick. Here it met the trackway from Berwick, and coaches then continued along the stretch of the present footpath, passing comp Barn, down Winton Street to Longbridge, and straight up the hillside and over Windover Hill. A couple of slight diversions avoided the steepest gradients, but horse-drawn coaches passed above the Long Man of Wilmington, and then turned to travel through Jevington and on to the old town of Eastbourne. When strong winds blew and the rain beat down, such a journey was obviously dangerous, but follow the route on foot (it is easily done from Berwick to the 700ft high top of Windover) and judge for yourself. In May 1780 Mary Capper, who was staying at

Wilmington, set out to Lewes, and she wrote in her diary: 'We walked as far as Longbridge, and it was fortunate that we did, as the road thither was so bad that the poor horses could not keep their legs. It was with much difficulty that four or five men who saw the embarrassment of the driver could release the chaise and one of the horses from a deep hole. We got in at Longbridge and proceeded very well – the road from there is remarkably fine.'

Edna and 'Mac' McCarthy; The Cuckmere *(1981)*

The Road Beneath the Downs

We've already met The Four Men *on page 11. In this extract Belloc lovingly traces the route under the Downs – a winsome stretch of road to this day. Bob Copper was later to walk it for his reprise* Across Sussex with Belloc.

So all along the road under Chanctonbury, that high hill, we went as the morning broadened: along a way that is much older than anything in the world: a way that leads from old Pevensey Port through the Vale of Glynde and across Cuckmere and across Ouse, and then up to the height of Lewes, and then round the edge of the Combe, and then down on to the ledge below the Downs, making Court House and Plumpton Corner, West Meston, Clinton, and Hollow Pie Combe (though between these two it branches and meets again, making an island of Wolstonbury Hill), and then on by Poynings and Fulking and Edburton, and so to the crossing of the water and the fort of Bramber, and so along and along all under the Downs until it passes Arun at Houghton Bridge, and so by Bury and Westburton, and Sutton and Duncton, Graffham and Cocking, and Diddling and Harting – all Sussex names and all places where the pure water having dripped through the chalk of the high hills, gushes out in fountains to feed that line of steadings and of human homes. By that way we went, by walls and trees that seemed as old as the old road itself, talking of all those things men talk of, because men were made for speech and for companionship, until we came to to the cross-road at Washington.

Hilaire Belloc; The Four Men *(1912)*

Underhill Lane

I've a fondness for Ruth Cobb's book about a part of Belloc's journey, because it's the part I know best. Indeed, I once lived at the very spot mentioned here, where a walker must decide whether to continue on the Ditchling Road or fork off along Underhill Lane.

I could see that the road I had travelled along seemed to turn sharply to the north at Westmeston, under shady trees, leaving the line of the Downs behind. That was not the direction which I meant to take; I wanted to follow the old track all the way to my destination: that track, surely, must run somewhere under the Downs.

There seemed to be nobody about of whom I could ask the way: it is extraordinary how deserted the country can still be at certain times of the day. The only living thing in sight was a strange dog which ignored me. Then, fortunately, a boy came through the gate of a farmyard.

'Where does the main road lead to?' I asked him.

'Ditchling.'

'But after that? I want to reach Clayton.'

'You'll come to it past Ditchling.'

'But there must be another way, closer to the Downs.'

'There's only Under Hill Lane.'

Under Hill Lane! I liked the sound of that: that was certainly the road for me. The boy pointed over his shoulder to what I had thought was a track that merely led to a farm. I turned my back on the main road, and the boy called after me: 'If you want Ditchling, you are going the wrong way,' but I paid no heed.

It was quite obvious that I had found the direction I wanted. It was a narrow lane, only half the width of the road I had travelled up to the present: it did not look wide enough for a big farm cart to pass along it; but it followed the curve of the Downs, and I was seeing them as they who had first worn the track had seen them. I did intend to go to Ditchling, because, although it lies a little way off the early track, it is still part of the story of the road. I meant to approach it, not by the main road, but by one made by the Romans – a continuation of the one that ran from their encampment above, on down the steep side of the Beacon.

The sun was lighting up the hollows of the Downs, the effect changing every minute as I walked along. There seemed to be many ancient quarries, now overgrown with grass, and mounds of many queer shapes, some perhaps prehistoric barrows, others earth that had been thrown up from the quarries.

I realised that I was seeing Ditchling Beacon for the first time, the greatest height of this range of the Downs, 813 feet. It must be a great viewpoint, and it was singularly impressive, I thought, as I gazed from below. Probably primitive man fortified that height; the Romans certainly saw the value of the position, and did so. Many a beacon must have been lit there on days of rejoicing and victory. I had known that the main road to Ditchling might be built upon, almost in the way of a conventional suburb, as it reached the town, and that was one reason why I wished to avoid it; but I did not expect to find in this piece of lane with the delightful name some modern dwellings – they came as a shock.

I soon passed them, and for a while I was alone with the hills, until I came to farm buildings perched on the bank, on my left. I saw a narrow, muddy, leafy path on my right running north, and wondered whether it was one of the paths that had been used at night by the smugglers; many had come across the Downs about here, I knew. It looked to be impassable at present. Farther away I could see a group of red roofs, clustering below the short spire of a church – that must be Ditchling.

I was close enough now to the Beacon to see the Roman track, known as Ditchling Bostall, taking its zigzag course like a mountain-way down its steep side. it looked from here as if it would be impossible for heavy vehicles to go up and down it. But I knew that they had done so all through the ages; that it had been in the past the ancient coach road between Brighthelmstone and London, and that the ascent had been nothing for the tanks and motor vehicles of recent times.

Ruth Cobb; A Sussex Highway (1946)

A Forgotten Way

Walter Wilkinson got to know Sussex in unusual circumstances. He spent a spring and summer pushing a barrow along its byways, looking for pitches (and appreciative crowds) for his Punch and Judy show.

The weather was set perpetually fine, and I went on over Graffham common in a blaze of sunlight and radiant heat. A difficult road this for a pedestrian, as green ways over the common invite one from the road, and the dark pines, with shade and resinous odour, call one from the heated tar. Consequently the morning is passed in a few miles of tramping, and a good deal of dallying.

Graffham is a straggling village under the Downs, and the public road comes to an end there. It is not at all a satisfactory village for a passing showman; organisation and the hotch-potch of business being more necessary than the art of puppet-showing for the exploiting of those scattered but delightful cottages and houses. But if I did not get many pennies there was the camp in the field with the peewits, and, at night, a sight of the full moon riding over the darkly luminous Downs.

There can be no more-forgotten road in the country than the way to Heyshott, and if you woud sense for a moment country life as it was a hundred years ago then make your solitary way by the quiet road over the high, bare common, watch the farm boy riding, bareback, his runaway plough horse, and so down to the far away, forgotten village of old cottages, small and old, set about the spacious but rough-and-tumble green. The guide-books will tell you that Richard Cobden was born there, and you can only believe that busy man took all its energy away with him, and left the husk to lie among the fields under the Downs, to go on calmly with its agricultural ways, the same now as then, shabby, unprofitable, but full of quietness and beauty, and something bigger altogether than that knowing and ephemeral little economic stratagem which, at all events, did not prevent those lucky Victorian manufacturers from being the richest in the world.

Even the return to the railway station at Selham did not dispel the forgotten out-of-the-world feeling of this corner of Sussex. The station stands among the fields, and the passengers alight on the wooden platform, go out to the road with their bags and bundles, and melt away singly, mysteriously, into the lanes for unseen, far away houses.

Walter Wilkinson; A Sussex Peep-Show (1933)

An Old Highway

There is a spot on the southern edge of the Weald where, all unnoticed by the dusty traffic of the London Road, a gate gives access from the main highway to a broad lane between two hedges. So little is it used that there are no cart-ruts, save for the first few yards, and yet this was once a main road. Long since deserted, for this reason and that, the busy wheels no longer enter here; yet the distance between the hedges testifies that at one time it was no more by-road. Now great oaks stretch out their arms from either side to touch fingertips overhead, and buttercups, rushes and long grass flourish beneath.

Presently it passes a shallow pool where, perhaps, in bygone days the wagon-horses used to drink. The pond is now almost choked with water-weeds, and a huge old oak – with memories doubtless of busier days – leans thoughtfully over the brink. Anon the trees roof in the track completely and, in the quiet gloom, a riot of chervil and stinging nettle has arisen from the damp ground. One move into the sunshine and here is a typical Sussex hedgerow. At present the sunny side is a bold colour scheme in magenta and blue, for the red campion and forget-me-not are both in luxuriant bloom along the ditch which borders the path. It might seem daring to introduce yet another bright tint into such a combination, but no such scruples trouble the orange-tip butterfly as it dances along the warm rays.

Thus the old highway leads pleasantly along till one reaches an open space, and there, all around, lie masses of green clouds, of varying shades, but all delicate – the great forest of the Weald.

Richard Gilbert, 'The Old Highway' from Everyman's Sussex (1927)

An Ode to a Road

The most unlikely local best-seller of the millennium year was a Dutchman's encomium for a road many people would scratch their heads to place. The A272 starts near Heathfield in the east, and winds its way comfortably across the Hampshire border.

The A272 is only marginally special as a road. But for some reason it always filled me with a sense of nostalgia when we came across it or when I saw it on a map. It's a bit like falling in love and trying to explain why in a level-headed and rational way. I could argue that it is a country road exactly 90 miles long. Your map may give a slightly different figure, but drive it and you'll see that I am right: it's 90 miles. A gross of kilometres: 144. Nice figures, but so what? I could also argue that it runs almost exactly east-west. It wraps itself round the fifty-first degree of latitude in a most sensuous manner. That may be a bit rare, but it's nothing to write home about, let alone a book. I could argue that it is in the south of England, not too far from London. Not bad at all, of course. Far enough from the capital to be in the country, close enough to have ties with London. It's not too far away from the continent either. Is that good? I could also say that it runs between two ranges of hills: the North Downs and the South Downs. Ah, that's a bit better. That tells us that we might expect to see some lovely scenery.

But what is perhaps most special or surprising about the A272 is that it seems to go on all the time. Looking at it on a map you see it going in the direction of a certain town or another road as if it was going to stop there, but then looking at the other side it appears to go on again, often slightly more to the south or to the north. That happens lots of times. This road continually survives itself. For ninety miles it keeps cropping up again, coming back undefeated. A tenacious whole-hogger. But all these reasons put together would not provide a valid excuse for writing a book about it.

Here follows the real reason. I had this vague idea when I started my investigations, but now I know for certain. With hindsight I can unequivocally say why I have come to love this road. It represents England. It epitomises England. It's England in short. It captures the Englishness of English life.

Pieter Boogaart; A272 An Ode to a Road (2000)

7 · NOVEL APPROACHES

Sussex has appeared in countless works of fiction, sometimes peripherally but often almost as a character in its own right. Our first example, despite the chapter title, is a from a short story rather than a novel. Rudyard Kipling is the one writer of genius to have written extensively about the county, and 'They' is an excellent introduction to his short stories for readers not yet fortunate enough to have come across them.

Motoring through Sussex

One view called me to another; one hill-top to its fellow, half across the county, and since I could answer at no more trouble than the snapping forward of a lever, I let the county flow under my wheels. The orchid-studded flats of the East gave way to the thyme, ilex and grey grass of the Downs; these again to the rich cornland and fig trees of the lower coast, where you carry the beat of the tide on your left hand for fifteen level miles; and when at last I turned inland through a huddle of rounded hills and woods I had run myself clean out of my known marks. Beyond that precise hamlet which stands godmother to the capital of the United States, I found hidden villages where bees, the only things awake, boomed in eighty-foot lindens that overhung grey Norman churches; miraculous brooks diving under stone bridges built for heavier traffic than would ever vex them again; tithe-barns larger than their churches, and an old smithy that cried out aloud how it had once been a hall of the Knights of the Temple. Gipsies I found on a common where the gorse, bracken and heath fought it out together up a mile of Roman road; and a little farther on I disturbed a red fox rolling dog-fashion in the naked sunlight.

As the wooded hills closed about me I stood up in the car to take the bearings of that great Down whose ringed head is a landmark for fifty miles across the lower countries. I judged that the lie of the country would bring me across some westward-running road that went to his feet, but I did not allow for the confusing veils of the woods. A quick turn plunged me first into a green cutting brim-full of liquid sunshine, next into a gloomy tunnel where last year's dead leaves whispered and scuffled about my tyres. The strong hazel stuff meeting overhead had not been cut for a couple of generations, at least, nor had any axe helped the moss-cankered oak and beech to spring above them. Here the road changed frankly into a carpeted ride on whose brown velvet spent primrose-clumps showed like jade, and a few sickly, white-stalked bluebells nodded together. As the slope favoured I shut off the power and slid over the whirled leaves, expecting every moment to meet a keeper; but I only heard a jay, far off, arguing against the silence under the twilight of the trees.

Rudyard Kipling, 'They' (1904)

One End Street

Eve Garnett lived in Lewes, and (as this brief description makes clear) her children's novel is set in the town, although she chose to call it Otwell. There are, alas, no cinemas in Lewes today.

The Ruggles family lived in a small town – that is to say, there were three cinemas and Woolworth's five minutes' walk from their door, but no green fields without a sign of a house and just a hedge and trees all round, unless they walked for half an hour. The Town was called Otwell, except on the Railway Station and in advertisements where it was called 'Otwell-on-the-Ouse'. This was misleading, as many a visitor, lured from London in the summer by posters of the Ouse with Otwell and its famous Castle rising from the banks, had discovered.

For, in reality, the Ouse, a muddy sort of stream, flowed through the fields to the sea, six miles off, some way outside the Town; there was one place where it curved in, as if out of curiosity to see what the Town was like, and that was just beyond the station, so that it was really only the Railway Bridge and signal box that could truthfully be said to be 'on the Ouse', and the Railway Company made the most of this.
Eve Garnett; The Family from One End Street (1937)

Gay and Gaudy Brighton

Brighton has been the favourite Sussex location for novelists, as the next few entries suggest. Thackeray's work was published shortly after the coming of the railways – bringing the town, as he writes, within easy reach of the capital.

Some ten days after the above ceremony, three young men of our acquaintance were enjoying the beautiful prospect of bow windows on the one side and blue sea on the other, which Brighton affords to the traveller. Sometimes it is toward the ocean – smiling with countless dimples, speckled with white sails, with a hundred bathing-machines kissing the skirt of his blue garment – that the London looks enraptured: sometimes, on the contrary, a lover of human nature rather than of prospects of any kind, it is towards the bow windows that he turns, and that swarm of human life which they exhibit. From one issue the notes of a piano, which a young lady in ringlets practises six hours daily, to the delight of the fellow-lodgers: at another, lovely Polly, the nurse-maid, may be seen dandling Master Omnium in her arms: whilst Jacob, his papa, is beheld eating prawns, and devouring the *Times* for breakfast, at the window below. Yonder at the Misses Leery, who are looking out for the young officers of the Heavies, who are pretty sure to be pacing the cliff; or again it is a City man, with a nautical turn, and a telescope, the size of a six-pounder, who has his intrument pointed seawards, so as to command every pleasure-boat, herring-boat, or bathing-machine that comes to, or quits, the shore, etc. etc. But have we any leisure for a description of Brighton? for Brighton, a clean Naples with genteel lazzaroni – for Brighton, that always looks brisk, gay and gaudy, like a harlequin's jacket – for

Brighton which used to be seven hours distant from London at the time of our story; which is now only a hundred minutes off; and which may approach who knows how much nearer, unless Joinville comes and untimely bombards it.

William Makepeace Thackeray; Vanity Fair *(1848)*

Mrs Pipchin's Lodging House

In which the young Charles Dombey is sent to Brighton for his schooling and lodges with one of Dickens' vigorously drawn minor characters.

This celebrated Mrs Pipchin was a marvellous ill-favoured, ill-conditioned old lady, of a stooping figure, with a mottled face, like bad marble, a hook nose, and a hard grey eye, that looked as if it might have been hammered at on an anvil without sustaining any injury. Forty years at least had elapsed since the Peruvian mines had been the death of Mr Pipchin; but his relict still wore black bombazeen, of such a lustreless, deep, dead, sombre shade, that gas itself couldn't light her up after dark, and her presence was a quencher to any number of candles. She was generally spoken of as 'a great manager' of children; and the secret of her management was, to give them everything that they didn't like, and nothing that they did – which was found to sweeten their dispositions very much. She was such a bitter old lady, that one was tempted to believe there had been some mistake in the application of the Peruvian machinery, and that all her waters of gladness and milk of human kindness had been pumped out dry, instead of the mines.

The Castle of this ogress and child-queller was in a steep bye-street of Brighton; where the soil was more than usually chalky, flinty, and sterile, and the houses were more than usually brittle and thin; where the small front-gardens had the unaccountable property of producing nothing but maigolds, whatever was sown in them; and where snails were constantly discovered holding on to the street doors, and other public places they were not expected to ornament, with the tenacity of cupping-glasses. In the winter time the air couldn't be got out of the Castle, and in the summer time it couldn't be got in. There was such a continual reverberation of wind in it, that it sounded like a great shell, which the inhabitants were obliged to hold to their ears night and day, whether they liked it or no. It was not, naturally, a fresh-smelling house; and in the window of the front parlour, which was never opened, Mrs Pipchin kept a collection of plants in pots, which imparted an earthy flavour of their own to the establishment. However choice examples of their kind, too, these plants were of a kind peculiarly adapted to the embowerment of Mrs Pipchin. There were half-a-dozen specimens of the cactus, writhing round bits of lath, like hairy serpents, another specimen shooting out broad claws, like a green lobster; several creeping vegetables, possessed of sticky and adhesive leaves; and one uncomfortable flower-pot hanging to the ceiling, which appeared to have boiled over, and tickling people underneath with its long green ends, reminded them of spiders – in which Mrs Pipchin's dwelling was uncommonly prolific, though perhaps it challenged competition still more proudly, in the season, in point of earwigs.

Charles Dickens; Dombey and Son *(1848)*

Brighton Rock

Graham Greene's novel opens with a vivid description of Bank Holiday crowds arriving in Brighton, but this is matched by the following evocation of a race day in the town further on in the book.

It was a fine day for the races. People poured into Brighton by the first train. It was like Bank Holiday all over again, except that these people didn't spend their money; they harboured it. They stood packed deep on the tops of the trams rocking down to the Aquarium, they surged like some natural and irrational migration of insects up and down the front. By eleven o'clock it was impossible to get a seat on the buses going out to the course. A negro wearing a bright striped tie sat on a bench in the Pavilion garden and smoked a cigar. Some children played touch wood from seat to seat, and he called out to them hilariously, holding his cigar at arm's length with an air of pride and caution, his great teeth gleaming like an advertisement. They stopped playing and stared at him, backing slowly. He called out to them again in their own tongue, the words hollow and unformed and childish like theirs, and they eyed him uneasily and backed farther away. He put his cigar patiently back between the cushiony lips and went on smoking. A band came up the pavement through Old Steyne, a blind band playing drums and trumpets, walking in the gutter, feeling the kerb with the edge of their shoes, in Indian file. You heard the music a long way off, persisting through the rumble of the crowd, the shots of exhaust pipes, and the grinding of the buses starting uphill for the racecourse. It rang out with spirit, marched like a regiment, and you raised your eyes in expectation of the tiger skin and the twirling drumsticks and saw the pale blind eyes, like those of pit ponies, going by along the gutter.

In the public school grounds above the sea the girls trooped solemnly out to hockey: stout goal-keepers padded like armadillos; captains discussing tactics with their lieutenants; junior girls running amok in the bright day. Beyond the aristocratic turf, through the wrought-iron main gates they could see the plebeian procession, those whom the buses wouldn't hold, plodding up the down, kicking up the dust, eating buns out of paper bags. The buses took the long way round through Kemp Town, but up the steep hill came the crammed taxicabs – a seat for anyone at ninepence a time – a Packard for the members' enclosure, old Morrises, strange high cars with family parties, keeping the road after twenty years. It was as if the whole road moved upwards like an Underground staircase in the dusty sunlight, a creaking, shouting, jostling crowd of cars moving with it. The junior girls took to their heels like ponies racing on the turf, feeling the excitement going on outside, as if this were a day on which life for many people reached a kind of climax. The odds on Black Boy had shortened, nothing could ever make life quite the same after that rash bet of a fiver on Merry Monarch. A scarlet racing model, a tiny rakish car which carried about it the atmosphere of innumerable roadhouses, of totsies gathered round swimming pools, of furtive encounters in by-lanes off the Great North Road, wormed through the traffic with incredible dexterity. The sun caught it: it winked as far as the dining-hall windows of the girls' school. It was crammed tight: a woman sat on a man's knee, and another man clung on the running board as it swayed and hooted and cut in and out uphill towards the downs. The woman was singing, her voice faint and disjointed through the horns, something traditional about brides and bouquets, something which went with Guinness and oysters and the old

Leicester Lounge, something out of place in the little bright racing car. Upon the top of the down the words blew back along the dusty road to meet an ancient Morris rocking and receding in their wake at forty miles an hour, with flapping hood, bent fender and discoloured windscreen.

Graham Greene; Brighton Rock *(1938)*

Ragged Trousered Philanthropists

Robert Noonan, writing as Robert Tressell, died three years before his only novel was published. He'd be delighted to know that his anti-capitalist diatribe has become a minor classic of socialist literature. Mugsborough is, in an afterword, said to be some distance from the sea, but there's no doubt that it was based on Hastings – the town in which he settled in his early thirties, working as a sign-writer and house painter.

The town of Mugsborough was governed by a set of individuals called the Municipal Council. Most of these 'representatives of the people' were well-to-do retired tradesmen. In the opinion of the inhabitants of Mugsborough, the fact that a man had succeeded in accumulating money in business was a clear demonstration of his fitness to be entrusted with the business of the town.

Consequently, when that very able and successful man of business Mr George Rushton was put up for election to the Council he was returned by a large majority of the votes of the working men who thought him an ideal personage . . .

These Brigands did just as they pleased. No one ever interfered with them. They never consulted the ratepayers in any way. Even at election times they did not trouble to hold meetings: each one of them just issued a kind of manifesto setting forth his many noble qualities and calling upon the people for their votes: and the latter never failed to respond. They elected the same old crew time after time . . .

The Brigands committed their depredations almost unhindered, for the voters were engaged in the Battle of Life. Take the public park for instance. Like so many swine around a trough – they were so busily engaged in this battle that most of them had no time to go the park, or they might have noticed that there were not so many costly plants there as there should have been. And if they had inquired further they would have discovered that nearly all the members of the Town Council had very fine gardens. There was a reason for these gardens being so grand, for the public park was systematically robbed of its best to make them so.

There was a lake in the park where large numbers of ducks and geese were kept at the ratepayers' expense. In addition to the food provided for these fowl with public money, visitors to the park used to bring them bags of biscuits and bread crusts. When the ducks and geese were nicely fattened the Brigands used to carry them off and devour them at home. When they became tired of eating duck or goose, some of the Councillors made arrangements with certain butchers and traded away the birds for meat.

One of the most energetic members of the Band was Mr Jeremiah Didlum, the house-furnisher, who did a large hire system trade. He had an extensive stock of second-hand furniture that he had resumed possession of when the unfortunate would-be purchasers failed to pay the instalments regularly. Other of the second-hand things had been purchased for a fraction of their real value at Sheriff's sales or from people whom misfortune or want of employment had reduced to the necessity of selling their household possessions.

Another notable member of the Band was Mr Amos Grinder, who had practically monopolised the greengrocery trade and now owned nearly all the fruiters' shops in the town. As for the other shops, if they did not buy their stocks from him – or, rather, the company of which he was managing director and principal shareholder – if these other fruiterers and greengrocers did not buy their stuff from his company, he tried to smash them by opening branches in their immediate neighbourhood and selling below cost. He was a self-made man: an example of what may be accomplished by cunning and selfishness.

Then there was the Chief of the Band – Mr Adam Sweater, the Mayor. He was always the Chief, although he was not always Mayor, it being the rule that the latter 'honour' should be enjoyed by all the members of the Band in turn. A bright 'honour', forsooth! to be the first citizen in a community composed for the most part of ignorant semi-imbeciles, slaves, slave-drivers and psalm-singing hypocrites.

Robert Tressell; The Ragged Trousered Philanthropists *(1914)*

The Light Over the Coast

George Moore has fallen out of fashion, but his tale of a young kitchenmaid ruined by the cook's wordly son is a fine novel – with the additional attraction, for our narrow purposes, of having large parts of it set in Sussex.

She was glad of the chance to get a mouthful of fresh air, and William held the hunting gate open, which she had never been through before, and was surprised to find herself in front of so much wild country: two great ranges of downs – the Shoreham Downs in front of them, rising up hill after hill as if the earth had once aspired to reach the sky; the Worthing range, some miles away, over against the great shallow valley of the Adur, full of green water meadows and long herds of cattle.

There was a smell of sheep in the air, and the flock trotted past them in good order, followed by the shepherd, with a huge hat on his head, a crook in his hand, and two shaggy dogs at his heels. A brace of partridges rose out of the sainfoin, and flew down the hills; and watching their curving flight Esther and William saw the sea under the sun-setting and the string of coast towns.

'A lovely evening, isn't it?'

Esther acquiesced; and tempted by the warmth of the grass they sat down.

'We shan't have any rain yet awhile.'

'How do you know?'

'I'll tell you,' William answered, eager to show his superior knowledge. 'Look due south-west, straight trough that last dip in them line of hills. Do you see anything?'

'No, I can't see nothing,' said Esther, after straining her eyes for a few moments.

'I thought not . . . Well, if it was going to rain you'd see the Isle of Wight.'

For something to say, and hoping to please, Esther asked him where the racecourse was.

'Over yonder. I can't show you the start, a long way behind that hill, Portslade way; and then they come right along by that gorse and finish up by Truly barn. You can't see Truly barn from here – that's

Thunder's barrow barn; they go quite a half a mile farther.'

'And do all that land belong to the Gaffer?'

'Yes, and a great deal more, too; but this downland isn't worth much – not more than about ten shillings an acre.'

'And how many acres are there?'

'Do you mean all that we can see?'

'Yes.'

'The Gaffer's property reaches to Southwick Hill, and it goes north a long way. I suppose you don't know that all this piece that lies between us and that barn yonder once belonged to my family.'

'To your family?'

'Yes, the Latches were once big swells; in the time of my great-grandfather the Barfields couldn't hold their heads as high as the Latches. My great-grandfather had a pot of money, but it all went.'

'Racing?'

'A good bit, I've no doubt. A rare 'ard liver, cock-fighting, 'unting, 'orse-racing from one year's end to the other. Then after 'im came my grandfather; he went to the law, and a sad mess he made of it – went stony-broke and left my father without a sixpence; that is why mother didn't want me to go into livery. The family 'ad been coming down for generations, and mother thought that I was born to restore it; and so I was, but not as she thought, by carrying parcels up and down the King's Road.'

Esther looked at William in silent admiration, and feeling that he had secured an appreciative listener, he continued his monologue regarding the wealth and rank his family had formerly held, till a heavy dew forced them to their feet, and they followed the paths through the furze, stopping to listen to a nightingale in the coombe below.

'In that thorn tree over yonder – don't you see?' he said.

The coast began to light up soon after, and William pointed out Brighton, Portslade, Southwick, Shoreham, Lancing and Worthing.

The sheep had been folded, and seeing them lying between the wattles, the greyness of this hill-side, and beyond them the massive moonlit landscape and the vague sea, Esther suddenly became aware, as she had never done before, of the exceeding beauty of the world.

George Moore; Esther Waters *(1894)*

Local Elections in Rye

E.F. Benson lived at Lamb House in Rye (Tilling in his novels) and was mayor from 1934-37 – at the time when Lucia's Progress *was published. He wrote several novels featuring the spiteful Miss Elizabeth Mapp and her arch rival, Lucia, all full of recognisable local detail.*

The result of the poll was declared two mornings later with due pomp and circumstance. The votes had been counted in the committee room of the King's Arms Hotel in the High Street, and thither at noon came the Mayor and Corporation in procession from the Town Hall clad in their civic robes and preceded by the mace-bearers. The announcement was to be made from the first floor balcony overlooking the High Street. Traffic was suspended for the ceremony and the roadway was solid with folk, for Tilling's interest in the election, usually of the tepidest, had been vastly stimulated by the mortal rivalry between the two lady candidates and by Irene's riotous proceedings. Lucia and Georgie had seats in Diva's drawing-room window, for that would be a conspicuous place from which to bow to the crowd: Elizabeth and Benjy were wedged against the wall below, and that seemed a good omen. The morning was glorious, and in the blaze of the winter sun the scarlet gowns of Councillors, and the great silver maces dazzled the eye as the procession went into the hotel.

'Really a very splendid piece of pageantry,' said Lucia, the palms of whose hands, despite her strong conviction of success, were slightly moist. 'Wonderful effect of colour, marvellous maces; what a pity, Georgie, you did not bring your paint-box. I have always said that there is no more honourable and dignified office in the kingdom than that of the Mayor of a borough. The word "mayor" I believe, is the same as Major – poor Major Benjy.'

'There's the list of the Mayors of Tilling from the fifteenth century onwards painted up in the Town Hall,' said Georgie.

'Really! A dynasty indeed!' said Lucia. Her fingers had begun to tremble as if she was doing rapid shakes and trills on the piano. 'Look, there's Irene on the pavement opposite, smoking a pipe. I find that a false note. I hope she won't make any fearful demonstration when the names are read out, but I see she has got her dinner-bell. Has a woman ever been Mayor of Tilling, Diva?'

'Never,' said Diva. 'Not likely either. Here they come.'

The mace-bearers emerged on to the balcony, and the Mayor stepped out between them and advanced to the railing. In his hand he held a drawing-board with a paper pinned to it.

'That must be the list,' said Lucia in a cracked voice.

The town-crier (not Irene) rang his bell.

'Citizens of Tilling,' he proclaimed. 'Silence for the Right Worshipful the Mayor.'

The Mayor bowed. There were two vacancies to be filled, he said, on the Town Council, and there were seven candidates. He read the list with the number of votes each candidate had polled. The first two had polled nearly three hundred votes each. The next three, all close together, had polled between a hundred and fifty and two hundred votes.

'Number six,' said the Mayor, 'Mrs Emmeline Lucas. Thirty-nine votes. Equal with her, Mrs Elizabeth Mapp-Flint, also thirty-nine votes. God save the King.'

He bowed to the assembled crowd and, followed by the mace-bearers, disappeared within. Presently the procession emerged again, and returned to the Town Hall.

'A most interesting ceremony, Diva. Quite mediaeval,' said Lucia. 'I am very glad to have seen it. We got a wonderful view of it.'

E.F. Benson; Lucia's Progress (1935)

Joanna Godden

Born at St Leonards on Sea in 1887, Sheila Kaye-Smith was one of the leading 'regional' authors of her day, and was widely known as 'the Sussex writer' since she based her novels almost exclusively in the county. The setting for Joanna Godden is Little Ansdore Farm on Wallands Marsh, three miles from Rye. A 'looker' was a shepherd.

It struck her that she had timed her visit a little too late. Already the brightness had gone from the sunset, leaving a dull red ball hanging lustreless between the clouds. There was no wind, but the air seemed to be moving slowly up from the sea, heavy with mist and salt and the scent of haws and blackberries, of dew-soaked grass and fleeces . . . .

Socknersh stood before her with his blue shirt open at the neck. From him came a smell of earth and sweat . . . . his clothes smelt of sheep.

She opened her mouth to tell him that she was highly displeased with the way he had managed her flock since the shearing, but instead she only said:

'Look!'

Over the eastern rim of the marsh the moon had risen, a red, lightless disk, while the sun, red and lightless too, hung in the west above Rye Hill. The sun and the moon looked at each other across the marsh, and midway between them, in the spell of their flushed, haunted glow, stood Socknersh, big and stooping, like some lonely beast of the earth and night . . . A strange fear touched Joanna – she tottered, and his arm came out to save her . . . .

It was as if the marsh itself had enfolded her, for his clothes and skin were caked with the soil of it . . . . She opened her eyes, and looking up into his, saw her own face, infinitely white and small, looking down at her out of them. Joanna Godden looked at her out of Socknersh's eyes. She stirred feebly, and she found that he had set her a little way from him, still holding her by the shoulder, as if he feared she would fall.

'Do you feel better, missus?'

'I'm all right,' she snapped.

'I beg your pardon if I took any liberty, missus. But I thought maybe you'd turned fainty-like.'

'You thought wrong' – her anger was mounting – 'I trod on a mole-hill. You've messed my nice alpaca body – if you can't help getting dirt all over yourself you shouldn't ought to touch a lady even if she's in a swound.'

'I'm middling sorry, missus.'

His voice was tranquil – it was like oil on the fire of Joanna's wrath.

'Maybe you are, and so am I. You shouldn't ought to have cotched hold of me like that. But it's all of a match with the rest of your doings, you stupid great owl. You've lost me more'n a dozen prime sheep by not mixing your dip proper – after having lost me the best of my ewes and lambs with your ignorant notions – and now you go and put finger marks over my new apalca body, all because you won't think, or keep yourself clean. You can take a month's notice.'

Socknersh stared at her with eyes and mouth wide open.

'A month's notice,' she repeated, 'it's what I came her to give you. You're the tale of all the parish with your ignorance. I'd meant to talk to you about it and give you another chance, but now I see there'd be no sense in that, and you can go at the end of your month.'

'You'll give me a character, missus?'

'I'll give you a prime character as a drover or a poughman or a carter or a dairyman or a housemaid or a curate or anything you like except a looker. Why should I give you eighteen shillun a week as my looker – twenty shillun as I've made it now – when my best wether could do what you do quite as well and not take a penny for it? You've got no more sense or know than a tup . . .'

She stopped, breathless, her cheeks and eyes burning, a curious ache in her breast. The sun was gone now, only the moon hung flushed in the foggy sky. Socknersh's face was in darkness as he stood with his back to the east, but she could see on his features a look of surprise and dismay which suddenly struck her as pathetic in his helpless stupidity. After all, this great hulking man was but a child, and he was unhappy because he must go, and give up his snug cottage and the sheep he had learned to care for and the kind mistress who gave him sides of bacon . . . There was a sudden strangling spasm in her throat, and his face swam in the sky on a mist of tears, which welled up in her eyes as without another word she turned away.

His voice came after her piteously.

'Missus – missus – but you raised my wages last week.'

Sheila Kaye-Smith; Joanna Godden (1921)

Cold Comfort Farm

If the beast-like Socknersh in the above entry is reminiscent of any other literary character it is probably one of those denizens of the rundown Sussex farm in Stella Gibbons' comic masterpiece. This is no accident: Gibbons was lampooning not the country folk themselves, but just the kind of novel that Sheila Kaye-Smith was writing.

Dawn crept over the downs like a sinister white animal, followed by the snarling cries of a wind eating its way between the black boughs of the thorns. The wind was the furious voice of this sluggish animal light that was baring the dormers and mullions and scullions of Cold Comfort Farm.

The farm was crouched on a bleak hill-side, whence its fields, fanged with flints, dropped steeply to the village of Howling a mile away. Its stables and out-houses were built in the shape of a rough octangle surrounding the farm-house itself, which was built in the shape of a rough triangle. The left point of the triangle abutted on the farthest point of the octangle, which was formed by the cowsheds, which lay parallel with the big barn. The out-houses were built of rough-cast stone, with thatched roofs, while the farm itself was partly built of local flint, set in cement, and partly of some stone brought at great trouble and enormous expense from Perthshire.

The farm-house was a long, low building, two-storied in parts. Other parts of it were three-storied. Edward the Sixth had originally owned it in the form of a shed in which he housed his swineherds, but he had grown tired of it, and had it rebuilt in Sussex clay. Then he pulled it down. Elizabeth had rebuilt it, with a good many chimneys in one way and another. The Charleses had let it alone; but William and Mary had pulled it down again, and George the First had rebuilt it. George the Second, however, burned it down. George the Third added another wing. George the Fourth pulled it down again.

By the time England began to develop that magnificent blossoming of trade and imperial expansion which fell to her lot under Victoria, there was not much of the original building left, save the tradition that it had always been there. It crouched, like a beast about to spring, under the bulk of Mockuncle Hill. Like ghosts embedded in brick and stone, the architectural variations of each period through which it had passed were mute history. It was known locally as 'The King's Whim'.

The front door of the farm faced a perfectly inaccessible ploughed field at the back of the house; it had been the whim of Red Raleigh Starkadder, in 1835, to have it so; and so the family always used to come in by the back door, which abutted on the general yard facing the cowsheds. A long corridor ran half-way through the house on the second story and then stopped. One could not get into the attics at all. It was all very awkward.

Growing with the viscous light that was invading the sky, there came the solemn, tortured-snake voice of the sea, two miles away, falling in sharp folds upon the mirror-expanses of the beach.

Under the ominous bowl of the sky a man was ploughing the sloping field immediately below the farm, where the flints shone bone-sharp and white in the growing light. The ice-cascade of the wind leaped over him, as he guided the plough over the flinty runnels. Now and again he called roughly to his team:

'Upidee, Travail! Ho, there, Arsenic! Jug-jug!' But for the most part he worked in silence, and silent were his team.

Stella Gibbons; Cold Comfort Farm *(1932)*

Chalkhill Blue

East Dean and neighbouring Crowlink, although not named as such, were the settings for the first of a series of highly praised novels by Richard Masefield, who farms not far away. The nation is preparing for war . . .

Down the coast at Newhaven, the Channel ferries were requisitioned as troop carriers and auxiliary warships, and the port itself entrusted with a primary role in the transport of stores and munitions to France. On the downs around Seaford huge army camps were established to train troops in all aspects of infantry warfare – and to electrify the prim little resort with mass nude bathing from its beaches.

In the wake of the shocking news that Liege had fallen to the enemy, a flood of homeless Flemish refugees had descended on boarding houses and private homes in Eastbourne and Brighton and other large coastal resorts. And everywhere committees and sub-committees sprouted like field mushrooms at the end of a wet summer – a War Refugees Committee, a Committee for Red Cross Supplies, War Savings and War Distress Fund committees, and the euphemistically named 'Emergency Committee' – charged with preparations for a possible German invasion of Sussex. Daily newspaper reports of events across the Channel were uncertain, out-of-date and hopelessly confusing. Stirring accounts of Belgium's heroic defence made each engagement sound like a victory. Yet manifestly the German host was continuing to advance.

In the absence of any more defnite instruction, there was nothing for Ned and his men to do, however, but to heed the Government's demands for increased agricultural production, and to prepare for the coming Sheep Fair.

Sellington Sheep Fair was the single event in the farming calendar to which the entire population of the valley was still committed. For this one day the eyes of several counties were to be focused on them – and the responsibility was keenly felt. For the weeks running up to the event Helen Ashby was busy turning out Useful and Fancy Work for the traditional Bury bric-`a-brac stall, working with clumsy persistence in the media of pipe-cleaners, seashells, rochet, lacquiered fir-cones and passe-partout. Up in the village the cottagers were also hard at work. Drunken cabbages were staked upright, yellowing onion-tops combed into line, curtains laundered, windows cleaned and polished with newspaper, and every item on the shelves of Pilbeam's Post office and Stores laboriously dusted and replaced. At the Lamb Inn a special consignment of Tipper Ale was ordered well in advance from the brewery at Newhaven for the greatest influx of the drinking year. And down in Sellington Meadow the area laid-off for the cricket pitch was freshly mown and rolled.

One way or another most of the other old village fairs had fallen by the wayside in recent decades. Less land under the plough meant less folding, fewer sheep on the hills; while cheap New Zealand lamb and rail access to the great sheep fairs of Lewes and Chichester had made cross-country droving less of a profitable proposition. But Sellington Fair survived. In the days of Ned's great-grandfather, Jonas Ashby, it had been a purely local event – a time at the end of the shepherd's year for the eastern downland flockmasters to foregather to exchange rams and cull surplus ewes, and sell off store tegs for fattening. But in Sellington's case the coming of the railways in the eighteen forties had actually brought new buyers for Southdown stores from the big arable farms to the north and the west. Sellington's position at a junction of chalk ridgeways that now linked it with the railway goods yard of Eastbourne, Polegate and Seaford had ensured not only its survival, but its expansion.

Richard Masefield; Chalkhill Blue (1983)

8 · FROM THE HORSE'S MOUTH
Letters, diaries & memoirs

What people write privately isn't necessarily to be trusted, especially if they have an eye to posterity, but there's often a sharper, less guarded quality in evidence. Certainly Gideon Mantell, the Lewes-based geologist who discovered the bones of an iguanadon near Balcombe, would have tempered his view of the Earl of Sheffield's artworks had he been writing for the public prints. The historian Edward Gibbon was befriended by the Earl, who brought his body to Sussex after his death in 1794 and had it interred in the Sheffield mausoleum in Fletching church. The house, overlooking Sheffield Park Gardens, is now divided into private luxury apartments.

Poor Taste at Sheffield Place

May 21st, 1821

Visited the Earl of Sheffield, and was much amused by looking over his lordship's house. There is some good modern stained glass with armorial bearings. A fine painting . . . of an Angel presenting the spirit of a child before the Almighty (this his lordship values at one thousand guineas) and some good portraits; but no other pictures of consequence; in fact the bulk of the paintings were mere rubbish, and unworthy house room. Gibbon's bedroom continues in statu quo as in his lifetime, the bed, chairs, pictures etc, everything remains the same; I felt a sensation of melancholy pleasure as I viewed these relics of the Historian of Rome: the room was decorated with portraits of Gibbon and of his relatives. A bedroom which was formerly occupied by the Princess of Wales (the present Queen) is still reserved as a state chamber: a fine and excellent portrait of her majesty is placed in the dressing room adjoining.

Sheffield Place is most romantically situated in a fine park, amidst a whole assemblage of oaks and elms: the pleasure grounds are very picturesque; but the most enchanting spot is a noble glen well wooded on both sides, and a fine lake of water at the bottom. We walked to this place, which is a mile or more from the house, and penetrated the wood till we came to a cottage, most enchantingly placed in a little recess of the sandstone, overhung by majestic beech, oak and ash: it is certainly one of the most romantic spots in our county: we returned by passing round the head of the lake, and thus reached the opposite bank, which if possible was more enchanting than the other. We partook of a syllabub and returned home.

The Journal of Gideon Mantell

John Cowper Powys at Court House

Some critics feel that his autobiography was the best thing Powys ever wrote. Here he writes about the time he spent near Offham at the beginning of the twentieth century.

Court House was an isolated farmhouse on the north side of the high downs, just under Mount Harry, and not far from Ditchling Beacon. On this inland side of these steep downs there lies that lovely touch of wooded and pastoral country known as the Weald. Here, not very far from the Ditchling Road, were several dedicated haunts for anyone who like myself resembled a wandering wild-duck in his mania for lonely rushy meres and the solitary pond-waters of moated granges!

But I had not to go as far as these romantic spots to find a place where I could enjoy my misanthropic solitude. Just below Court House, on the outskirts of the Weald, there was a wonderful wood, of oaks and hazels and elms and beeches, called by the Walter-de-la-

Mare name of 'Waringore'. To this would I would almost daily repair, and penetrating into the centre of it walk up and down a narrow mossy path, strewn with rubble and fallen twigs and old dead leaves, and sprinkled in autumn by crimson toadstools and in spring by white violets. Perhaps the most ideal of all my daily walks to my taste would be a narrow path through a hazel wood *on perfectly flat ground* that went on and on for three or four miles! I remember perfectly well thinking to myself as I trod this path through Waringore, that whatever was happening to me in life, just to be able to stare at this green moss, at these fallen twigs, at those blood-stained funguses, was sufficient reward for having been born upon this cruelty-blasted planet!

But, as I say, within a few miles of us were even more romantic spots than Waringore Wood. Of course when I make an effort to conjure up all these spirit-memories what I get back are simply certain imaginative and visual impressions. I completely forget names! There was one extraordinary old place – half manor house, half ancient mill – that we used often to visit, quite near the Ditchling Road, but I rather think the other side of Plumpton, whose name totally escapes me. There was an ancient church, too, with an enormous yew tree, that always had an unusual number of red fairy yew berries on it, somewhere, it seems to me, by the side of a large pond in the middle of wide-stretching woods.

Before we left Court House we made several very exciting expeditions into various neighbouring villages – anywhere within a radius of five or six miles – with a vague idea of changing our abode; for it was an unsatisfaction sensation, you must understand, never to set eyes on the orb of the sun, no! not in the height of the summer, after two o'clock in the afternoon! Some of the most vivid of all my mysterious floating, drifting, suddenly-appearing, suddenly-vanishing islands of memory come back to me from these wayfarings. Aerial fragments of scenery they are, *landscape-revenants*, materialised for a second and then withdrawn once they came. Images they are of half-seen roadways, parcels of woodland, portions of wagon-rutted lanes descending between primrose banks, isolated patches of village-greens, with muddy duck ponds, angry geese, croaking frogs . . . these visions come floating along the airways of my mind in clear distinctness, not like aquarelles or pastels, not like ancient oil paintings. Nor are their margins blurred, nor are their roots, in those mental air spaces, left trailing, nor are they edges vague or their shapes ruffled; and yet all their horizons are dark, so dark that when they vanish, they vanish without leaving a trace behind!

John Cowper Powys; Autobiography (1934)

Virginia Woolf Visits Charleston

A corner of East Sussex is for ever Bloomsbury. Virginia Woolf bought Monk's House at Rodmell (now owned by the National Trust), while her sister Vanessa lived with her fellow painter Duncan Grant and a flexible cast of other artists and writers at Charleston Farmhouse, near Firle. Virginia loved her sister, but not uncritically.

March 5, 1919

Charleston is by no means a gentleman's house. I bicycled round there in a flood of rain, & found the baby asleep in its cot, & Nessa & Duncan sitting over the fire, with bottles & bibs & basins all round them. Duncan went to make my bed. Their staff at the moment consists simply of Jenny, the sharp Jewish looking cook; & she having collapsed, spent the afternoon in bed. By extreme method & unselfishness & routine on Nessa's and Duncan's parts chiefly, the dinner is cooked & innumerable refills of hotwater bottles & baths supplied. One has the feeling of living on the brink of a move. In one of the little islands of comparative order Duncan set up his canvas, & Bunny wrote a novel in a set of copy books. Nessa scarcely leaves the babies room, or if she appears for a moment outside, she had instantly to go off & talk to Dan, Jenny's young man & the future support of Charleston, or to wash napkins, or bottles, or prepare meals. Mrs B. & the children run rapidly to and fro between their rooms. I had an immense long talk with Ann [Brereton] about the health of the Persian cat, which according to Mrs B. was fatally injured internally while being washed to cure it of nits; so that she demanded chloroform, which Nessa refused, & the cat recovered. Then Quentin had just been suspected of measles. The atmosphere seems full of catastrophes which upset no one; the atmosphere is good humoured, lively, as it tends to be after three months of domestic disaster. In these circumstances, I dare say I had no more than 30 minutes consecutive talk with Nessa, chiefly devoted to the great epic of the Dr the nurse and Emily. But as it happens after disaster upon disaster a sudden lightening of calamity appeared this morning: Dan & his mother being engaged, a letter then arrived from a nurse who against all probability seems to wish to come if she may bring a friend. But I broke off in full tide, & had to trudge through mud to Glynde – such mud that when I went into Powell, the land agent, the sleek little clerk looked from my head to my boots in expostulation – as if such a figure couldn't possibly require a house with 7 bedrooms & a bathroom. Unhappily there seems little chance of finding one. I've said nothing to my niece, who must be called so formally since they've cancelled Susanna Paula, & can think of nothing else. She is a wistful, patient, contemplative little creature, examining the fire very meditatively, with a resigned expression, & very large blue eyes. I suppose not much larger than a big hare, though perfectly formed – legs, thighs, fingers & toes – both fingers & toes very long and sensitive.

The Diaries of Virginia Woolf, Vol I 1915-1919 (1977)

Bloomsbury Sisters

The niece in the above entry, born on the previous Christmas Day, was eventually named Angelica. She was Vanessa's daughter by Duncan Grant rather than her husband, Clive Bell. Bunny Garnett, seen writing a novel when she was born (and at one time Duncan's lover), later married her – archetypal Bloomsbury. Angelica was hurt by not learning of her parentage until she was seventeen, but her memoirs are warm, rather than bitter, and beautifully written.

It was at teatime that I remember Virginia's arrival at Charleston, pacing through the house, followed by Leonard and Pinka, the spaniel, whose feathered pads would slap on the bare boards beside her master's more measured footfall. Virginia, seeing myself and Vanessa sitting by the fire or under the apple tree in the garden, would crouch beside us, somehow finding a small chair or low stool to sit on. Then she would demand her rights, a kiss in the nape of the neck or on the eyelid, or a whole flutter of kisses from the inner wrist to the elbow, christened the Ladies' Mile after the stretch of sand in Rotten Row, Hyde Park, where Vanessa in the past had ridden on a horse given her by George Duckworth.

Virginia's manner was ingratiating, even abject, like some small animal trying to take what it knows is forbidden. My objection to being kissed was that it tickled, but I was only there to be played off against Vanessa's mute, almost embarrassed dislike of the whole demonstration. After a long hesitation, during which she wished that some miracle would cause Virginia to desist, she gave her one kiss solely in order to buy her off. Although she felt victimised and outwitted by her sister, she won the day by her power of resistance, and an utter inability to satisfy Virginia's desires, which completely disregarded Vanessa's feelings. She suffered mainly because, much as she loved Virginia and deep though her emotions were, she became almost unbearably self-conscious when called upon to show them. Of her love for Virginia there was no question: she simply wished that it could have been taken for granted. They were both affectionate, but Virginia had the advantage of articulateness, which Vanessa may have distrusted, having suffered from it in the past: Virginia's flashes of insight into other people's motivations could be disturbing. In one word she could say too much, whereas Vanessa, priding herself on her honesty, was inclined to say too little. Neither could Vanessa compete with Virginia's brilliance and facility; made to feel emotionally inadequate, she also imagined herself lacking in intelligence. She distrusted Virginia's flattery, in which she detected an element of hypocrisy, setting her on a pedestal for false reasons, but she did not see how to retaliate without brutality, of which she was incapable. She became more and more truculent, her exasperation masked by an ironic smile with which she tried to discourage Virginia's efforts to extract a sign of love.

Angelica Garnett; Deceived with Kindness (1984)

John Evelyn Greets his Wife

The diarist John Evelyn, born in 1620, was sent to Lewes as a young boy to live with his mother's father and stepmother, the Stansfields: (his grandfather largely financed South Malling church, and the lad

laid one of the first stones). In 1647, escaping the civil war in Paris,
he contracted to marry Mary Browne, then just thirteen, attracted by
'the pretynesse and innocence of her youth' and 'a Gravity I had not
observed in so tender a bud'. Five years later the time came to
welcome her to England.

1652 3rd June.
I received a letter from Colonel Morley to the Magistrates and
Searchers at Rye, to assist my wife at her landing, and show her all
civility.

4th. I set out to meet her now on her journey from Paris, after she
had obtained leave to come out of that city, which had now been
besieged some time by the Prince of Condé's army in the time of the
rebellion, and after she had been now near twelve years from her own
country, that is, since five years of age, at which time she went over. I
went to Rye to meet her, where was an embargo on occasion of the
late conflict with the Holland fleet, the two nations being now in war,
and which made sailing very unsafe.

On Whit Sunday I went to the church (which is a very fair one) and
heard one of the canters, who dismissed the assembly rudely, and
without any blessing. Here I stayed till the 10th with no small
impatience, when I walked over to survey the ruins of Winchelsea,
that ancient cinq-port, which by the remains and ruins of ancient
streets and public structures, discovers it to have been formerly a
considerable and large city. There are to be seen vast caves and vaults,
walls and towers, ruins of monasteries and of a sumptuous church, in
which are some handsome monuments, especially of the Templars,
buried just in the manner of those in the Temple at London. This place
being now all in rubbish, and a few despicable hovels and cottages
only standing, hath yet a Mayor. The sea, which formerly rendered it
a rich and commodious port, has now forsaken it.

11th June. About four in the afternoon, being at bowls on the green,
we discovered a vessel which proved to be that in which my wife was,
and which got into the harbour about eight that evening, to my no
small joy. They had been three days at sea, and escaped the Dutch
fleet, through which they had passed, taken for fishers, which was
great good fortune, there being seventeen bales of furniture and other

rich plunder, which I bless God came all safe to land, together with my wife, and my Lady Browne, her mother, who accompanied her.

The Diary of John Evelyn

Provoked to Folly

The East Hoathly shopkeeper Thomas Turner kept a now celebrated diary, no small part of its entertainment value lying in the consequences of his low resistance to alcohol: the very first entry ends, typically, 'Went to bed drunk'.

February 22nd, 1758

About 1.10 Mr French sent his servant with a horse for my wife, who accordingly went with him and dined at Mr French's. Myself and family at home dined on the remains of Wednesday's supper and a dish of cheap soup. Tho. Davy dined with us in order to taste our soup. About 6.40 I walked down to Whyly, where we played at brag the first part of the even; myself and wife won 1s 2d. About 10.20 we went to supper on 4 boiled chickens, 4 boiled ducks, some minced veal, sausages, cold roast goose, cold chicken pasty, cold ham, damson and gooseberry tarts, marmalade and raspberry puffs. Our company was Mr and Mrs Porter, Mr and Mrs Coates, Mrs Atkins, Mrs Hicks, Mr Piper and his wife, Joseph Fuller and his wife, Tho. Fuller and his wife, Dame Durrant, myself and wife and Mr French's family. After supper our behaviour was far from that of serious, harmless mirth, for it was downright obstreperous mirth mixed with a great deal of folly and stupidity. Our diversion was dancing (or jumping about) without a violin or any music, singing of foolish and bawdy healths and more such-like stupidity, and drinking all the time as fas as could be well poured down; and the parson of the parish was one amongst the mixed multitude all the time, so doubtless in point of sound divinity it was all harmless. But if conscience dictates right from wrong, as doubtless it sometimes does, mine is one that we may say is soon offended. For I must say I am always very uneasy at such behaviour, thinking it is not like the behaviour of the primitive Christians, which I imagine was most in conformity to our Saviour's gospel. Nor would I on the other hand be thought to be either a cynic or a stoic, but let social improving discourse pass around the company. But, however, about 3.30, finding myself to have as much liquor as would do me good, I slipped away unobserved, leaving my wife to make my excuse; for sure it was rude, but still ill-manners are preferable to drunkenness (though I was far from being sober). However, I came home, thank God, very safe and well without ever tumbling or any other misfortune, and Mr French's servant brought my wife home at about 5.10 . . .

Thursday 23rd Feb. This morn about 6 o'clock, just as my wife was gladly got to bed and had laid herself down to rest, we was awakened by Mrs Porter, who pretended she wanted some cream of tartar. But as soon as my wife got out of bed, she vowed she should come down, which she complied with and found she, Mr Porter, Mr Fuller and his wife with a lighted candle, part of a bottle of wine and a glass. Then the next thing in course must be to have me downstairs, which I being apprised of, fastened my door. But, however, upstairs they came and threatened as also attempted to break open my door, which I found they would do; so I therefore ordered the boys to open it. But as soon as ever it was open, they poured into my room, and as modesty forbid me to get out of my bed in the presence of women, so I refrained. But their immodesty permitted them to draw me out of bed (as the common phrase it) tipsy turvy. But, however, at the intercession of Mr Porter they permitted me to put on my breeches (though it was no more than to cast a veil over what undoubtedly they had before that time discovered); as also, instead of my clothes, they gave me time to put on my wife's petticoat. In this manner they made me dance with them without shoes or stockings until they had emptied their bottle of wine and also a bottle of my beer. They then contented themselves with sitting down to breakfast on a dish of coffee etc. They then obliged my wife to accompany them to Joseph Durrant's, where they again breakfasted on tea etc. They then all adjourned to Mr Fuller's where they again breakfasted on tea, and there they also stayed and dined; and about 3.30 they all found their ways to their respective homes, beginning by that time to be a little serious, and in my opinion ashamed of their stupid enterprise, or drunken perambulation. Now let anyone but call in reason to his assistance and seriously reflect on what I have before recited, and they must I think join with me in thinking that the precepts delivered from the pulpit on Sundays by Mr Porter, though delivered with the greatest ardour, must lose a great deal of their efficacy by such examples. Myself and family at home dined on the remains of yesterday's dinner. Mr Jordan called on me but did not stay. Mr Elless and Joseph Fuller in the evening called in to ask me how I did after my fatigue and stayed and smoked a pipe with me. And so this ends the silliest frolic as I think I ever knew, and one that must cast an odium on Mr and Mrs P. and Mrs F. so long as it shall be remembered.

Thomas Turner; The Diary of Thomas Turner 1754–1765

William Blake's Defence

We have discovered William Blake enjoying Felpham (page 74), but the poet's stay in Sussex was marred by his trial for sedition and assault in Chichester. He was supposed to have uttered the words 'Damn the king, damn his soldiers' and 'When Bonaparte comes I'll help him'. These were troubled times politically, but it does seem ludicrous that the charges weren't thrown out at an early stage. Although Blake was acquitted, this letter to his friend Thomas Butts was written when the outcome was far from certain.

August 16, 1803

I am at Present in a Bustle to defend myself against a very unwarrantable warrant from a Justice of Peace in Chichester, which was taken out against me by a Private in Captn. Leath's troop of 1st of Royal Dragoons, for an assault and seditious words. The wretched Man has terribly Perjur'd himself, as has his Comrade: for, as to Sedition, not one Word relating to the King or Government was spoken by either him or me. His Enmity arises from my having turned him out of my Garden, into which he was invited as an assistant by a Gardener at work therein, without my knowledge that he was so invited. I desired him, as politely as was possible, to go out of the Garden; he made me an impertinent answer. I insisted on his leaving the Garden; he refused. I still persisted in desiring his departure; he then threaten's to knock out my Eyes, with many abominable imprecations & with some contempt for my Person; it affronted my foolish Pride. I therefore took him by the Elbows & pushed him before me till I had got him out; there I intended to have left him, but he, turning about, put himself into a Posture of Defiance, threatening & swearing at me. I perhaps foolishly & perhaps not, stepped out at the Gate, &, putting aside his blows, took him again by the Elbows, & keeping his back to me, pushed him forwards down the road about fifty yards – he all the while endeavouring to turn round & strike me, & raging & cursing, which drew out several neighbours. At length, when I had got him to where he was Quarter'd which was very quickly done, we were met at the Gate by the Master of the house, *The Fox Inn* (who is the proprietor of my Cottage) & his wife and Daughter & the Man's Comrade & several other people. My landlord compell'd the Soldiers to go in doors, after many abusive threats against me & my wife from the two Soldiers; but not one word of threat on account of Sedition was utter'd at that time. This method of Revenge was Plann'd between them after they had got together into the stable. This is the whole outline.

A Song for Every Season

We've seen Bob Copper going about his work as a barber's boy in trying circumstances (page 50), so let's retrace his steps to the years of innocence. His writing is superb, but he and his family are better known for their singing.

I remember as a small boy of about five lying on a heap of straw on the granary floor watching Grand-dad mend holes in an old corn-sack draped across his knee with a curved packing needle threaded with twine that smelt like turpentine. I lay there watching and listening intently as the ancient story unfolded, for the old man was singing, in a deep, resonant bass, a song he had heard from his own grandfather when he had been my age. The dog curled up beside me in the hot morning sunshine that slanted in through the large, open double doorway feigned sleep. Only the twitching of an ear or an occasional half-hearted attempt to wag his tail when Grand-dad's voice swelled to a higher note gave away the fact that he was alive to all that was going on.

I am quite sure I was not aware at the time of the full significance of such moments in my boyhood but somewhere deep down inside a chord of sympathy was being plucked which still rings clear to this day. That was over fifty years ago and it is by such slender threads as these that we are still connected with English village life of a couple of centuries ago.

That song is only one of many that our family have loved and kept alive down the years and now, in addition to the more durable things that remain in our village to remind us of days gone by – the church, the gaunt, black windmill on the ridge of the hill and the sturdy, flint farm-houses and barns built in the seventeenth century – we have something more fragile and far more likely to perish with the passing of the years than these monuments in stone and seasoned oak. It is something also that is more intimately connected with the lives of the villagers for, until comparatively recently, it has existed only in people's minds, having been handed down orally from one generation to another. We have a heritage of traditional songs.

Up until about the turn of the century these songs were sung frequently at the recurring village merry-makings that cropped up from time to time as the year ran its course. 'Spud-planting Night', sheep-shearing suppers and 'Hollerin' Pot' at harvest time gave the local songsters regular chancs to give voice to their favourites. But as other interests came along and the old men passed away there was a sharp decline in the number willing or able to sing the old songs and also in the opportunities for those remaining to do so.

Our family has always had a built-in love of these songs and has therefore been slower than most to forget them. In fact my father, Jim, made a determined effort to ensure that they would be remembered by writing down the words of over sixty of them in what he called his 'Song Book'. He did this in 1936 and I have always looked upon it as a legacy. He was a great songster. No matter where he was or what he was doing, if the job in hand was conducive to singing he seemed to find it went along easier with a song. When I was a boy we lived in a farm cottage at the north end of the village, and whether he was lighting the fire in the kitchen range in the morning, working at his carpenter's bench during the day or hoeing between his carrots and onions in his garden in the evening, he was seldom wthout a song on his lips. He was also a determined singer. A mere snatch of a verse here or an odd chorus there were just not good enough for him. Once he started a song he had to go on until he reached the end. This may have been due to the fact that many of them had a story, and having a tidy mind, he liked to see it carried through to its conclusion whether the subject was the farming year, a courtship or a battle at sea.

These songs were very old when he was a boy and although it is always difficult to date songs of this vintage with any certainty one could say that the majority of them are from a hundred to a hundred and fifty years old while some are very much older. They are the songs that used to be sung in Rottingdean, Sussex, by the men who struggled to lift a living from the shallow top-soil of the surrounding hill country or from the deep, salt-sea waves of the English Channel that almost lapped their doorsteps, and by the women who brought up huge families in the tiny cottages huddled together down in the High Street. In singing them they expressed their joys and sorrows, their hopes and fears and so the songs themselves reflect the way the villagers lived, loved, worked and played in those far-off days.

Bob Copper; A Song for Every Season *(1971)*

A Sussex Privy

The actor Dirk Bogarde was brought up in the Cuckmere Valley in the 1920s and 30s, his memories of his childhood recounted in two books, Great Meadow *and the first volume of his autobiography, extracted here.*

We walked along in silence for a bit; well, not really silence because she was doing one of her songs and I was whistling little bits here and there, in case she thought I was puffed. Which I was. At the top of the field the cottage roof stuck up with its chimney, and then the flint walls and the two rather surprised windows in the gable looking down to the farm. Round the cottage was a rickety wooden fence with bits of wire and an old bedstead stuck in it, and some apple trees and the privy with its roof of ivy and honeysuckle and a big elderberry. The privy had no door, so you just sat there and looked into the ivy; no one could see you through it, but *you* could see them coming along the little path and so you were able to shout out and tell them not to in time. It was really quite useful. And better than a door really, because that made it rather dark and a bit nasty inside. And once a bat got in there after Lally had closed it and she screamed and screamed and had a 'turn'. So we left off the door for summer and just sort of propped it up in the winter, to stop the snow drifting and making the seats wet.

There were three seats, like the Bears'. A little low one, a medium one, and the grown-up one. The wood was white and shining where we used to scrub it, and the knots were all hard and sticking up. No one ever used the smallest one, we had the paper and old comics and catalogues for reading in that; and the medium one just had a new tin bucket in it with matches and candles for the candlestick which stood on a bracket by the paper roll, and a cardboard tin of pink carbolic.

There were lids to all the seats, with wooden handles, and they had to be scrubbed too – but not as often as the seats; which was every day and a bit boring. Sometimes at night it was rather nice to go there down the path in the dark, with the candle guttering in the candlestick and shadows leaping and fluttering all around and the ivy glossy where the golden light caught it. Sometimes little beady eyes gleamed in at you and vanished; and you could hear scurrying sounds and the tiny squeaks of voles and mice; and once a hare hopped straight into the doorway and sat up and looked at me for quite a long time, which was fearfully embarrassing, until I threw the carbolic tin at him and he hopped off again.

Dirk Bogarde; A Postillion Struck by Lightning *(1977)*

Lewes During the War

Mrs Henry (Alice) Dudeney was for a time a fêted novelist, although her reputation had wilted by the end of her life. In 1998 Tartarus Press brought out a selection of her letters, edited by Diana Crook (A Lewes Diary 1916-1944), from which these extracts are taken. The first entry, written while she was recovering from the flu, tells of the one serious air raid suffered by Lewes during the Second World War.

20 January, 1943. At 12 when I was peaceful in bed, the most terrific bangs. The bed and house shook. I was stunned and so defenceless

undressed. Winnie came rushing up with some loving incoherence about 'dying together'! A plane rushed past the window, flying very low. The black shadow of it shut out the light. I shall always think of the Angel of Death and the 'beating of its wings'. I shall never see a blackbird fly past my window without remembering. Three more followed, very close and low; they seemed to be at the window pane. More bangs, rushings vibrations. I expected the house to go. Then silence. We learned later that 2 people were killed and many injured. . . We, and the Lucas's, have escaped with broken windows. Winnie came up with my supper at 9 and the news that they 'couldn't dig out poor old Mrs Digweed'. (They did in the end.)

22 January. The most awful devastation in the town, especially in North Street, New Street and New Road. The Stag Hotel burnt to the ground and Stevensons the corn chandler has lost his windows with almost the last lovely fanlights left in Lewes. All the people have got clear out of St Martin's Lane, which was also hit. I sat in my chair all day, half asleep, but jumping like a shot rabbit if even a cinder dropped out of the fire.

24 January. Caroline Byng Lucas. Might she come and paint this room tomorrow? Rang up – delighted; yes, of course.

25 January. What very nice women she and her sister Mrs Byng-Stamper are. She sat and painted till lunch time and I stayed in my bedroom by the electric fire. She, like all people of imagination, in *Despair* about everything. No *Freedom* left, nor any chance of it, war or no war. All elegance and charm, the things that *we* value, to be ruthlessly crushed out. They, she and her sister had difficulty in finding the money to buy the Newingtons' house in the High Street. But did and let the first two floors to the Red Cross and planned to start a School of Painting on the top floor. Suddenly their telephone rings. They are told that the whole house has been taken over by the East Sussex County Council and that it is useless to protest and to point out that the house belongs to them. '*You have no appeal.*' She now proposes to start her school in the stable at the bottom of the garden, but begs me not to say a word, because if they got wind of it they'd take that too! What nonsense to say we are fighting for Freedom. German rule could not be worse than this.

9 · ROUTES TO THE SEA

We have no mighty rivers in Sussex, but none of us lives far from one and most of us probably have a favourite stretch we like to visit. Where a river begins is open to interpretation (there are sometimes several minor tributaries), and writers of Sussex books are by no means always in agreement.

Our Patriotic Rivers

Anyone looking at the convolutions of the rivers on a map of Sussex must be struck with the way which they restrict themselves to the confines of the county. The depth of Sussex, from the north to the south, is not very extensive, but the Sussex rivers, with commendable local patriotism, a strong sense of the *genius loci*, however near to alien borders they may rise, are plainly determined to remain on Sussex territory. The course of the eastern Rother (there are two Rothers in Sussex) is particularly noticeable. It rises at Rotherfield – that great Sussex antiquary and historian, Mark Anthony Lower, records the curious and interest fact that 'the River Rother rises in the cellar of the mansion called Rother House in the parish of Rotherfield' – and swings due eastward through Etchingham straight to the borders of Kent, but there makes a sharp turn and with an angle like an elbow flows down to Rye and enters the sea below Winchelsea. A

river most obviously determined to remain in Sussex. The Ouse and
the Adur are faithful to the same ambition, and the Arun twists and
turns like a snake to contain her waters in the narrow stretch, but half
the depth of Sussex, between her junction with the western Rother
and her meeting with the sea at Littlehampton. Only one famous river
rises in Sussex and then deserts the county, and that is the Medway.

Sussex rivers are not noted for striking beauties – no gorges, rocks
or waterfalls adorn them, and the waters of East Sussex are inclined
to be muddy. There is a certain modesty in their scenic claims. But the
Arun offers enchanting pictures to memory, running under
overhanging beechwoods, or clear in the sunshine, or – perhaps most
magical of all – as seen from the high bluff of Burpham, meandering
along amid a thick embroider of reeds and rushes and willow herb,
with the romantic towers of Arundel Castle beyond. This is the Old
River Arun, and owes its lazy afternoon charm to the fact that the
main stream has been diverted to a more direct course.

Such a river scene is as different as possible from the Ouse at
Piddinghoe, with the broad slow stream washing the muddy banks,
some barge-like vessel lying at anchor, the whole plain, peaceful look
of the country thereabout. Above this rises the little eminence on
which is set the enchanting round-towered church of Piddinghoe, of
whose 'begilded dolphin' Kipling speaks – on the weather-vane is not
a dolphin but a salmon-trout; it must be admitted that Kipling's
version sounds much more poetical. . . The ouse was a salmon river
once.

The western Arun and the eastern Ouse, in the differing quality of
their aspect and character, typify the richness of West Sussex and the
austerity of East Sussex.

Esther Meynell; Sussex (1947)

The Winding Western Rother

Much of the history of Sussex is written on the banks of the Rother,
which rises at Greatham and courses deviously to join the Arun.
Indeed to explore the Rother is one of the most rewarding and
illuminating walks in the county as it makes its way through such
villages at Trotton, Iping, Stedham and Woolbeding. Through fields

where the past lies buried, once the 'Black Country' of Britain, where countless ploughmen have eaten cheese and bacon, and where more than one sovereign has hunted deer and banqueted. This is the river of Lord Camoys, who commanded a flank at Agincourt, and is buried in Trotton church, and of poor Otway, the Elizabethan playwright, who, when starving, choked to death on a morsel of bread. Another Elizabethan, Michael Drayton, watched these waters too.

The Rother has seen both the great and the lowly and all the shades in between, and a host of travellers have crossed its bridges. Rivers, like roads, have an affinity. They both go places, and all such ancient ways have their own identity. It was the river and its fording places that attracted the roads and brought its people. The river sustains, provides work and power and even now in the 20th century the Rother has retained a sense of timelessness, that elusive quality that is a necessity in a work of art. But a river does not stop moving and neither does time, and great changes have taken place on the Rother. To some people these changing patterns may have passed unnoticed, but they are none the less great, and an understanding of them will help us in the future when we weigh our values in exchanging new lamps for old. Once there were 13 watermills taking their power from the Rother to turn their great clacking wood and iron wheels. And now, this autumn (1966), Terwick Mill, the last of the Rother watermills, is closing down.

Bernard Price; Sussex: People, Places, Things (1975)

The Bridge at Stopham

This beautiful bridge is now free of traffic, thanks to the construction of a utilitarian modern structure alongside it. It's best enjoyed from the garden of the White Hart.

If the motorists on the Petworth road rush past Hardham Church unheeding, they have to change their pace and focus their attention on another ancient and lovely thing some three miles further west. This is the bridge over the Arun at Stopham. All artists who see it want to paint it. All poets want to sing its praises. Fortunately for the cause of Beauty, the turns of the road here are such that the bridge cannot be rushed at speed. Long may it be so. For this bridge at Stopham is one of the oldest and most beautiful of all the bridges of England, and it is in one of the loveliest pieces of river scenery that this land can show. Built six hundred years ago, of a stone mellowed by the palette of the centuries, the bridge is a delight in proportion. It is engaging in design, with its great buttresses and the quaint angles in the sides where the passing churls of Plantagent days had to squeeze themselves to avoid the cattle going to market or the brusque passage of men-at-arms. The passing walkers of today are also grateful to those angled niches to avoid the cars pursuing each other over that narrow way.

The river here is at its broadest and sweetest, slumbering in wide pools under the shade of the beech, the alder and the willow, the poplar and the birch, while in early summer the placid waters quiver with purple and crimson, reflecting the rhododendrons on the sides of the enfolding hills.

George Aitchison; Sussex (1936)

A Walk by the Adur

The Adur was once tidal as far upstream as Bramber, where there was a substantial bridge close to the medieval house, St Mary's.

I am out for the day. I intend to walk up the west side of the Adur as far as Beeding bridge, then find my way back along the eastern side of the waters. I know I shall see a great many things – far more than I have time and space to enter here. But then every day of our life, if only we are awake, is a crowded affair; concrete facts, impressions, musings, dreams, come to us innumerable and when, in memory, we look back it is only the mountain tops, or little else, that we recall.

I do not call the Adur a greatly winding river. There are no sinuosities such as we see at the Cuckmere, and wide coursings as on the Arun; it just moves with a slight wavering up to Beeding, and further on to Knepp Castle. The walk is not a considerable one on a long summer's day. Moreover, I am only going to skim the story of the walk, for every bend of the road shows something worth telling.

In days which are now very distant the river was wider, and had a fullness at floodtide even greater than it is now; it had wharves along its edges for fisher-folk and sailor-folk, and Domesday Book mentions salt pans and gives hints of tons and hams which, except for a few names, have entirely vanished. Rivers were the first highways of our land.

A.A. Evans; 'By the Adur River' from A Saunterer in Sussex *(1935)*

The Beginnings of the Ouse

Over 30 miles north and west of the busy little port of Newhaven, two tiny waterfalls splash on to the rocks of a tree lined hollow to form the accepted begining of our Sussex Ouse. The waterfalls flow from Slaugham millpond, covering 40 acres, and this in turn is fed by a spring and by the streams and waters of the man-made Slaugham furnace pond, standing 250 feet higher than the tidal waters of Newhaven harbour and created some 400 years ago as part of the Wealden iron industry. In the hollow below the mill pond a stream, measurable in inches, is formed, and it flows gently past the long abandoned ruins of Slaugham Place, under the busy A23 road and through an arch of the Balcombe Ouse Valley Viaduct. Thousands of commuters cross this viaduct each year, yet few spare a glance at the stream beneath. Fewer still notice the rush-filled area opposite, once the wharf for unloading from barges of bricks, stones and other materials used to build this viaduct.

South of Ardingly the stream swells to river proportions after being joined by waters from the new Ardingly reservoir, about 150 feet above sea level and today offering recreational facilities such as boating, fishing and nature trailing. This reservoir occupies the area where formerly Ardingly and Shell Brooks linked after flowing down from Wakehurst Place and Balcombe Mill. The Cockhaise Stream descends from the area of Horsted Keynes to further swell our river, which then wanders on its course, under the Bluebell Railway, round Sheffield Park and through Fletching and Newick to Isfield. Tributaries come from east and west, the Maresfield or Shortbridge Stream, the River Uck, the Bevern, the Longford and others. Flat water meadows flank the tree-lined Ouse as it winds to the well loved Barcombe Mills with its new reservoir, its fascinating series of bridges crossing mill stream, river, canal and fishing pools, its weirs and its locks converted into modern 'fish ladders'. High tides reach this point, and southwards the Ouse now changes character as salt water reacts on river bank vegetation. The old arm of the river winds around the peninsula topped by the picturesque Hamsey Church, lone sentinel of a long disappeared riverside settlement. Here the river is clearly tidal. More twists take the Ouse past Malling, and downland now stands high on three sides as the river heads towards the narrow gap in the chalk which gave to Lewes the strategic importance which made it for so long a principal town in Sussex.

Edna and 'Mac' McCarthy; Sussex River (1979)

A Hesitant Paean to the Sussex Ouse

There's a shortage of humour in topographical verse, so I'm pleased to include a wry view of the Ouse from a contemporary poet who loves it, but knows not to make grand claims.

It is really a very small river for something
That sends ferries daily to France.
It is, after all, about twenty miles long
And its width can't be said to enhance
Its portent. No, it's a modest affair
That will seldom say boo to a goose.
But this isn't Devon – it just wouldn't do
For these waters to dart fast and loose.
You can tell it has less than the self-esteem
Of the Garonne saluting Toulouse,
Or the breadth to make headway of cousin the Medway –
It isn't the sort poets choose.

Like its four shire companions it's also in short
Supply of that great money-spinner
Called heritage. This is no bad thing:
You lose sleep when you're onto a winner.
And what is the virtue of all that chalk
And mud clay with its caramel goos,
If it isn't to turn life into a siesta,

One uninterruptible snooze?
Where easing of oarsmen into canoes
Is for sloth, the river's own views
Lack barges and houseboats, the sound is of moos
Or birdsong. Cars aren't what it woos.

Sprung from the beacons of pineclump and heather,
Twenty ditch tributaries cut pale clay deep
Under the shade of beech, hazel, oak, birch,
Rowan, willow, holly – through their leaf heap
To clearings, from brambles to fern and bracken,
Emerald moss and foxgloves. The stream-heads
Of the forest, its brindle floor, chance to dwindle or
Meet into one to pass fields dipped like beds.

This might be why it can seem further shy,
Sheltered by broad leaves above;
Until it is feted in the gap it created –
It hugs Harvey's brewery with love.
Then it proceeds through the flat lands of reeds
And Virginia Woolf's last haunt –
To waft the swans to the forthcoming bay
And the shock of some ships to flaunt.

Robert Edwards; from Attitude to Sussex, *(1990)*

A Ravine-like Valley

Though the Cuckmere Valley divides two sections of the Downs, the division is less marked than the divisions made by the other three river valleys. The Cuckmere Valley is narrower and in some places almost ravine-like, so that often there are closely associated features on both sides of it, especially near or at the coast. For instance, Seaford Head on the west side of Cuckmere Haven is an integral part of the cliffs on the east side, where the Seven Sisters cliffs extend out in a long line to join the huge bulk of Beachy Head. The Cuckmere Valley and the Cuckmere River, the walls of the Downs rising abruptly west of the valley, and the hills folding away into the east, all merge together in natural harmony. Note that you do not say the River Cuckmere but always the Cuckmere River, and the first syllable is not pronounced as in 'cluck' but as in 'cuckoo'.

Nowhere in the whole range of the South Downs will you find finer scenery than among the hills and valleys and along the coast of this stretch of downland – for the seascape now becomes as important as the landscape. There are about thirty square miles of outstanding beauty, and more of it open to the walker than not. It enjoys several forms of protection, but it is under constant threat. The 'developers', of course, always have their eyes on it, and sometimes danger appears from sources which one should not need to fear. Councillors, for instance, have talked about the possibility of a 'scenic drive' along part of the escarpment and possibly elsewhere, but mercifully such nightmares have not reached reality. Landscapes such as these should be so conserved as to admit little or no alteration beyond necessary management. Scrub must be kept down, trees occasionally felled, the river cleared, farm buildings repaired or extended, and sometimes new ones built. But major introductions or alterations for the sake of that vague but extraordinarily comprehensive thing, amenity, should be firmly slapped down. Change does not necessarily bring improvement. Too often it brings the reverse.

One should take a prolonged pause at the place where the ridgeway meets the lip of the Cuckmere Valley, for this is one of three outstanding viewpoints in the region. Gazing across to Windover Hill on a clear day, with intermittent cloud and sunshine, I think of Robert Bridges rather than of Kipling:

O bold majestic downs, smooth, fair and lonely;
O still solitude, only matched in the skies:
    Perilous in steep places,
    Soft in the level races,
Where sweeping in phantom silence the cloudland flies.

Ben Darby; The South Downs (1976)

10 · THE TOWNS

Towns generally receive a poorer press than villages, but Sussex has many on a human scale and not entirely ruined by the inevitable spread of tarmac and concrete – among them our two county towns, Chichester and Lewes. We begin this chapter with an anonymous petition addressed to the Lord Treasurer of England.

Chichester in 1596

Right honorable, althoughe I am of the number that littel can profit the comonwealth, yet in wel wishing to my contry being second too none I am moved humbly too shewe unto your honor as followeth.

That the citty of Chichester doth so fast decay and run to ruine, and the multitude inhabiting there so fast growe too beggory that except for remedy thereof some speedy order bee taken it is very likely the multitude of poor in the liberty of that citty encreasing wil cause the better sorte (being fewe that can contribute towards the releefe of the poorer) by reason of charges to wex weery of inhabiting the citty: whereby the citty which is weake and ruinous wanting her people also wil become every way weake.

British Museum, Lansdowne MS.81 no 44

Chichester in 1635

A generation later the petitioner's wishes for 'some speedy order' seem to have taken effect. A Lieutenant Hammond was the man who travelled through 'the Western Counties'.

This little City (built by a Saxon King) stands sweetly in a pleasant fertile Levell, and not far from the maine Sea, her Buildings are indifferent, and her Streets fayre and cleane, especially those 4 cheife Streets that with the 4 Windes, runs streight along from the 4 Gates to the near, round-built Freestone Crosse, which stands in the very centre of this sweet little City, with 8 faire Arches, with statues round about, above curiously and artificially cutt and carv'd with the Crucifix on the top.

From G.G. Wickham Legg (ed), 'A Relation of a Short Survey of the Western Counties made by a Leiutenant of the Military Company in Norwich in 1635'; Camden Miscellany Vol XVI

Horsham in the early 18th century

John Warburton and the Rev John Burton both journeyed around Sussex in the early 1700s and left accounts of what they found. Warburton was a mapmaker, and therefore came here with an eye to business. Burton, visiting his stepfather, then rector of Shermanbury, made two tours, writing one account in Latin and the other in Greek.

I passed through the Forest of St Leonard which brought me to Horsham, a large straggling borough and town corporate in the figure of a cross and the streets called by the names of East, West, North and South Streets. The church is at the south end of the town and is a large edifice but irregular built and in bad repair. The steeple is a spire of a good height an covered with slate. The churchyard is near covered with frames of wood that are set over the graves and on them are various singular inscriptions. The Town House which stands in the Market Place is a good edifice of Portland stone supported by arched columns. . . At the north end of the Market Place stands the gaol built of freestone and crenellated on the top.

John Warburton

Thus far riding more than nine miles without dust indeed, but not without fatigue, we discovered on our right, close by, the lofty spire of a church, constructed of wood, but painted so as to resemble stone. This was the large and populous town of Horsham, the chief place in the Weald (formerly called the forest of Anderida) for here is the county gaol and sessions house; the natives come hither to attend the assizes once a year and to the market once a week and here the Londoners purchase vast quantities of poultry. I should not forget to mention that, in the midst of this muddy soil, a sandy eminence rises and continues for three miles, which we rode over with pleasure. Here too is another treasure, whose value here is enhanced by its scarcity. Here are quarries where they procure slate which serves to cover their houses instead of tiles and gives the town a respectable appearance.
Rev John Burton

Seaside Resorts in 1861

Black's Guide of 1861, recently reprinted in a fascimile edition by Country Books, gives a fascinating insight into the status of our resort towns a few decades after the spa craze had begun to transform them into fashionable watering places. The population figures themselves are statistics to wonder at. Brighton's 'black pitchy bricks' are mathematical tiles. 'Doctor Brighton' is the health-giving climate. As for Eastbourne, its growth had not yet begun.

BRIGHTON
Population, including Hove, 69,726. Average number of visitors 80,000. 'Brighton,' says Hazlitt, 'stands facing the sea, on the bare cliffs, with glazed windows to reflect the glaring sun, and black pitchy bricks shining like the scales of fishes. The town is, however, gay with the influx of London visitors – happy as the conscious abode of its sovereign! Everything here appears in motion – coming or going. People at a watering place may be compared to the flies of a summer; or to fashionable dresses, or suits of clothes, walking about the streets. The only idea you gain is of finery and motion.' Thackeray, in *The Newcomes*, writes of it more eulogistically: 'It is the fashion,' he says,

'to run down George IV; but what myriads of Lodoners ought to thank him for inventing Brighton! One of the best physicians our city has ever known is kind, cheerful, merry Doctor Brighton. Hail thou purveyor of shrimps, and honest prescriber of South Down mutton; no fly so pleasant as Brighton flys; nor any cliffs so pleasant to ride on; no shops so beautiful to look at as the Brighton gimcrack shops, and the fruits shops and the market.' Mr Thorne's graphic description will interest the reader: 'If some daring engineer were to lift the line of houses facing Park Lane, place them upon the south-coast railway, convey them to the seaside, and plant them directly alongside the beach, he would make an almost exact resemblance to Brighton as viewed from the sea. So much does the line of houses facing the cliff resemble some parts of the West End, that the spectator who has been shot down from town in an hour by the express train finds a difficulty in believing that he is far away removed from his old haunts, until he turns to the bright sea, which lies before him like a flat and polished mirror, and champing and frothing upon the pebbly beach below. The western extremity of the town, which is bounded by Adelaide Crescent and Brunswick Terrace and Square, lies comparatively low: and from this point to Kemp Town, which is fully 3 miles to the east, runs a splendid promenade. The life and variety which everywhere meet the eye along this pleasant walk is perhaps unequalled.' The great drawback of Brighton, however, is its *want of shade*. It has no trees to afford a coolsome shadow – no obscure groves, no romantic bowers.

EASTBOURNE

Eastbourne (population, 3033) covers a much larger extent of ground than its population would seem to necessitate. In fact, it consists of four different portions – the town, formed of four streets crossing each other almost at right angles; Sea Houses, a terrace overlooking the sands; Southbourne, three quarters of a mile from the sea, to the west of the station; and Meads, a small cluster of cottages and cornfields, about a quarter of a mile beyond Southbourne. The station is about midway between the town and Sea Houses. The roads like in the shadow of noble elms, and on each side stretch the green meadows and the smiling pasture. The walk along the sands to Beachy Head is one of unusual beauty . . .

Beachy Head (575 feet above the level) raises its glowing wall of chalk about 3 miles south-west of Eastbourne, and is a favourite excursion-point of the Eastbourne tourists. The prospect is sublime: eastward it extends to Dover, westward to the Isle of Wight. The shores of France may also be seen, it is said, on a cloudless day. But not for the mariner does this precipitous cliff wear so goodly an aspect. It is associated in his mind with tales of fearful wrecks – not so frequent now that our charts are more skilfully constructed, and the science of navigation is better understood, but still numerous enough to render Beachy Head 'a word of fear'. The Dalhousie, a fine East Indiaman, was lost here, October 24, 1853, and only one life was saved.

SEAFORD
Population 997. The old town was paced on the marge of the haven – formed by the junction of the Ouse with the Channel – which has been long filled up. The position, however, of the modern hamlet, with a bold sweep of sea before it, and lofty hills rearing their rounded crests behind it, is so picturesque that we may anticipate for it a long and prosperous career.

HASTINGS
Population, 21,215. 'We have been,' says Charles Lamb, 'dull at Worthing one summer, duller at Brighton another, dullest at Eastbourne a third, and are at this moment doing dreary penance at Hastings! I love town or country, but this detestable Cinque Port is neither. I hate these scrubbed shoots thrusting out their starved foliage from between horrid fissures of dusty innutritious rocks, which the amateur calls "verdure to the edge of the sea". I require woods, and they shew me stunted coppices. I cry out for the water-brooks, and pant for fresh streams and inland murmurs. I cannot stand all day on the naked beach, watching the capricious hues of the sea, shifting like the colours of a dying mullet. I am tired of looking out of the windows of this island prison. I would fain retire into the interior of my cage.' But the tourist will err woefully if he accepts Charles Lamb's delightful badinage for truthful description. Hastings is not only not a dull, but it is even a romantic and picturesque town, while it has enough of London comforts to satisfy the most fastidious Londoner. It has good

hotels, and good lodging-houses, and a German band, and a circulating library, an the shops are exceedingly smart, and the prices (in season) are aristocratically high!

WORTHING

Population 5,000. From a poor fishing village, it rose into sudden importance when George IV's patronage of Brighton attracted the attention of the fashionable world to the pleasures of sea-bathing and the beauties of the south coast. For their convenience an agreeable sea-walk or esplanade has been constructed, three-quarters of a mile in length. The sands extend their firm and pleasant surface for quite ten miles. The temperature is well adapted to invalids, the sea-scapes are beautiful, and the town is, in all respects, identical with other popular sea-side resorts.

BOGNOR

Bognor (population 1913) – i.e. the rocky coast – is Worthing's twin sister, a quiet, healthy watering-place, seated on a level, in face of the ever restless channel.

About 1786 Sir Robert Hotham, a wealthy Southwark hatter, determined upon acquiring the glory of a sea-side Romulus, and set to work to erect a town of first class villas in this pleasant spot, with a view of creating a truly *recherché* watering-place, to be known to posterity as 'Hotham town'. He spent £60,000, erected and furnished some commodious villas, but did not succeed in giving his name to his own creation, and died broken hearted in 1799. Fashion, however, after some slight delay, patronised the new English Bath, and Bognor grew by degrees into its present posterity.

Chichester Past and Present

To a stranger, taking superficial saunter through its streets, Chichester, cathedral city of the diocese, is after the pattern of most cathedral cities. You get the same impressions of the 'venerable pile', of the quiet cloisters, of smooth lawns and immemorial elms. There are pleasant discoveries of Gothic gateways leading from busy streets of prosaic shop-fronts and stuccoed walls to sequestered squares and lanes where comely Georgian and stately Queen Anne houses live in harmony with Tudor timberings and Plantagenet windows. yet the life of a bustling market town clatters and clangs through streets alternately of generous width and miserly narrowness. You will find the Cathedral and cloisters almost empty, save for those who use them professionally, and hardly a passer-by notes whether the windows are Early English or late bungaloid. The crowds are at the greengrocers, the garages, and in the shops of the various multiple stores, which seemed to have joined together in a vast conspiracy to make very town in England look exactly like the standardised London suburbs.

When, very young, very Puritan, very non-alcoholic, I made my first acquaintance with Chichester, in the nineteenth century, I was horrified. I had, till then, no conception that any town could contain so many breweries, so many dismal public houses, so many drunken people. The impression created on my youthful mind of stench and sordidness was such that for many years I avoided the city. Today, happily 'we have changed all that'. By 'we' I mean Chichester and I. 'I' because, in common with the rest of us as we have grown older, I have acquired buffers against shocks and superchargers for beauty. As for Chichester, I know that she has given herself a drastic clean-up.

George Aitchison; Sussex (1936)

Venerable East Grinstead

The whole district is served by East Gristead, near the Surrey border. This is a handsome and venerable town with a wide High Street, massive timber-framed walls, much Horsham slab roofing and a commanding, pinacled church tower completed in 1813. Its predecessor collapsed in 1785. East Grinstead is famous for the brilliant plastic surgery carried on at the Qeen Victoria Hospital. It is also memorable for the peace of Sackville Collge, founded by the second Earl of Dorset as almshouses and completed in 1619. It is considered one of the finest Jacobean buildings in the country. Not that there is anything splendid about it; what you remember is the dignity and the quiet repose.

In the twelfth century name Grenestlda we find again at echo of a forest clearing, a 'green place'. By about 1270 it had become

Estgrenested to distinguish it from Westgrenested (West Grinstead),
south of Horsham. Today East Grinstead is not only a good shopping
centre but also a popular commuter town for London. Once you
could also travel by rail from East Grinstead to Lewes; it was a single-
line railway and when I travelled on it, which was often, I used to
think of a parody somebody wrote of Wordsworth's poem:

> My heart leaps up when I behold
> A single railway line,
> For then I know the wood and wold
> Are almost wholly mine.

Wood, wold and quietness are all there still, but, alas, the little
railway fell a victim to 'economy' in 1955.

Ben Darby; View of Sussex *(1975)*

Quintessential Lewes

If the special place of the South Downs in our culture lies in its
recognition as a 'quintessentially English landscape', then Lewes is a
quintessential English town with its castle, former markets, coaching
inns and merchants' houses in their superb setting. It is the ony town
to lie in the heart of the Downs. As Graham Greene remarked, it is
both a hill town and a valley town which for long was a seaport. Not
the least of its attractions are glimpses caught from its steeply-
plunging lanes or from upper floors of houses in the long
thoroughfare of High Street. It is every bit as much a hill town as any
place that can be found in Tuscany and it is excactly the right size for
comfort. Its combination of medieval and Georgian domestic
architecture makes it a gem. Its population in 1700 appears to have
been no more than at Domesday Book in 1086 and even with its
modern growth it is really only a town in miniature. At the end of the
19th century William Morris viewed it 'lying like a box of toys under
a great amphitheatre of chalk hills'. This remains an apt description.
He also thought Lewes set fairer than any town he knew . . . Lewes
still retains something of its old character as a market town on which
converged once or twice a week within a radius of 10 miles or so the
inhabitants of the surrounding farms, villages, country houses,
vicarages and wayside cottages, after business at the market at The

Star (on the site of the town hall), the White Hart, or one of many other numerous inns. Lewes must now be one of the most beautiful small towns in England, but will it become 'chi-chi', as have the bogus towns of Surrey?

Peter Brandon; The South Downs *(1998)*

The Street Names of Crawley

When the village of Crawley was chosen as the site of a New Town immediately after the Second World War, someone had to decide on names for the hundreds of new roads that would be created. That man was John Goepel, who later produced a booklet which revealed his method – and his quirkiness.

Crawley had just been the subject of a boundary revision (the old limit ran down the middle of the High Street and the present Boundary Road) and we had taken over part of East Sussex, including Pound Hill. I thought 'What did William the Conqueror do when he took over England? – covered it with castles' – so I took for my first names the impressive list of Sussex castles. It was always my intention, so far as possible, to place roads in alphabetical order, working from the town centre outwards, so we have the castles Amberley, Bodiam, Camber and so on.

I had already decided to use Drive for the main approach road to a neighbourhood, with its suggestion of purposeful movement, and Avenue, the tree-lined route, carrying no development, for the roads separating the neighbourhoods. This choice has been well borne out by the glorious double line of flowering trees which now flanks Ifield Avenue, a quarter of a century after its naming.

The main road divided Langley Green into four sections, and I named them after birds, beasts, trees and no, not fishes – I did not want the tenants even subconsciously feeling that their houses were damp! On the edge of the area stood the house Old Martyrs, so I called the road to it Martyrs Avenue, and the closes leading off it after the best known martyrs: Stephen, the first martyr, on whose feast (26 December) Good King Wenceslas looked out; Beckett, to whose tomb the pilgrims set out from all over mediaeval England; Joan, the best known woman martyr, and Edmund.

In Southgate East I think I achieved my triumph and my downfall. I decided to use personal surnames which derive from the occupations of a rural Sussex community – baker, mason, wainwright etc, running as usual from the Town Centre outwards, and I was overjoyed to find that Brewer connected with the existing Malthouse Road, another link to help people find their way about. Shortly afterwards my wife was stopped in the street by a woman who asked 'Was is your husband who named the new roads?' Blithely she agreed. 'Well,' said her interlocutor, 'my friend finds she's living at the corner of Malthouse and Brewer Roads and she's secretary of the Temperance Association.'

Loriners, in case anybody is wondering, are iron workers, and wainwrights of course make waggons. Whether Fletchers carve up flesh or flight arrows can be argued. They fit among the Fs, with fishers and foresters.

In Tilgate I tried to commemorate famous Londoners, beginning with Dick Whittington, thrice mayor, and including, near the school, Colet, founder of St Paul's School, and Whitgift of Croydon school.

One section I dedicated to cathedrals, with the two access roads Canterbury and York, the seats of the archeipiscopates (what glorious polysyllables the Church can accumulate). The others are roughly in geographical location, Exeter in the west, Ely in the east, except that the Council substituted Chichester (which I was keeping for the County Buildings in the Town Centre) for my Chester. I exercised my ingenuity in putting a long name, Winchester, on a long road and a short one, Wells, on a short one; it helps the cartographer.

Every artist is allowed to sign his work, and I must confess that I put my own name at the bottom of the map of Crawley; in a cryptogram, of course. But just write the names Gloucester, Oxford, Exeter, Peterborough, Ely and Lincoln in a column and read the initial letters downward.

John Goepel; How I Chose Crawley Street Names (1990)

11 · THIS SPORTING LIFE

Although it produced, in C.B. Fry, one of the greatest all-rounders ever, Sussex has seldom excelled at sport – Brighton & Hove Albion's tenure among the footballing elite was all too brief, and although the county cricket side gloriously won the championship in 2003, this was for the very first time since its founding in 1839. But never mind: sport has been a passion for many, and it deserves celebrating here.

Cricket at Seaford

I remember one occasion, when my father, hearing that there was to be a match a Seaford between Public and Private School men, drove over to witness it.

On appearing on the ground he was at once seized upon by the Public School team, and entreated to play, as one of their number had at the last moment suddenly failed them. He pleaded that he had given over playing for many years. Then he pointed out a piece of water, which he said did not allow of a large enough field. Both sides laughed at the idea of the possibility of sending a ball as far as the water.

In the end my father was persuaded to play. When batting, on the first opportunity he had, he sent his ball into the middle of the sheet of water, where it could be seen floating about, and so could not be called a lost ball. On that ball my father obtained twenty-four runs, before anybody waded into the water after it.

Edward Boys Ellman, Recollections of a Sussex Parson *(1912)*

Cricket on Ice

A cricket match on the famous Sheffield Park lakes, which are coated with a covering of splendid ice was played on Saturday when, in compliance with that princely supporter of cricket, the Earl of Sheffield, Mr E.A. Bailey of Brighton took over a couple of elevens. . . . The ice was in magnificent condition for the latest venture, having a grand surface and a thickness of six inches . . . With the exception that no extras were counted and that a batsman was compelled to retire when he had made 20, the laws of the game governed the match. The allowance for a boundary hit (to the edge of the lake) was three.

Sussex Daily News, *February 1, 1895*

Cricket on the Common

Where, let me ask, is the Englishman who will not do homage to the noble game of cricket? Let us, by way of contrast to the present, look back at the game as played fifty years ago [1830] on our unenclosed common. That was the time for a merry day, when we challenged Hellingly, Chiddingly, Westham or any other parish, before clubs were known or thought of; when the honour of the parish was the object fought for; when churchwardens and overseers were patrons worth seeking and the curate would take the head of the table at the dinner or supper; when underhand bowling was the proper form, and before that innovator, Lillywhite, had introduced the break-shin overthrow; when white cord knee-breeches, white stockings showing off a good pair of calves, and tied shoes, with the chimney-pot hat, made up the swell cricketer's dress; before knee-pads, finger-pads or any other pads were known or thought of; when the game between parish and parish was pleasant to see, and one might take a part in the sport without danger to life or limb; when a good hearty all-round shout followed a good hit, and the company cheered the field for a difficult catch, and the man at the wicket shared the applause for taking, over the stumps, a well thrown-in ball.

'How's that?' he asked the umpire as the bails flew off. The wicket-keeper knew it was a nice point, but he thought it was out or he would not have put the question. The umpire hesitated, and appealed to his second-self, an old-fashioned farmer, and one who never did anything in a hurry.

'Can't say, really; was setting my watch by the church clock, so can't say zackly how 'twas.'

Of course, 'Not out' was the verdict.

In such pleasant ways in those old days did we settle our difficult points, and being in earnest, before the stumps were drawn the game would be played out. Tradesmen, farmers and respectable young fellows of all classes took part, together with our lawyer, who – being a crack hand – generally took the lead, and when a match was on the game would be played by our best men, victory alone being the aim. The dinner might be at stake with perhaps, in addition, pots and pints, winners and losers sharing equally in the liquor. There were few, if any, teetotallers in those old-fashioned days, with more familiarity between man and man and less drunkenness than at the present day.

Thomas Geering; Our Sussex Parish (1884)

A Handy Knife

The tale of a butcher's boy who had a flair for cricket – and wasn't stumped by adversity.

Unfortunately an elderly Clayton family were proving to be difficult with their meat deliveries, which meant I was often sent back to get their meat changed. 'Too fat!' was the cry. On this particular Wednesday I was due to play cricket in an away match departing at 1.30pm. In those days we travelled in Mr George Turner's lorry. The seats were made to enable them to be put in and removed quite easily. It was a bit of a shaky ride, but I looked forward to it.

On arrival at this customer I hoped the piece of steak would be satisfactory. I walked up the long garden path to the back door and knocked. After a short delay the door was opened by the daughter. I politely said 'Good morning,' but the good lady's first remark was not encouraging. 'It's too fat!' she said. Then, turning, she called out up the passage, 'Mother! The butcher is here, but it's fat again.'

'Bring it to me to look at,' I heard the mother call, and then she came shuffling out of a nearby room. She met the daughter, and after messing about and deliberating the old lady said 'It's too fat butcher, take it back.'

I was annoyed and hurried up the path to my bicycle and started to take the right fork of the road back to Ditchling. After cycling about 300 yards down the road I stopped, propped the cycle up by the hedge and, taking the offending meat (which meant cricket or no cricket) I sat down by a small pond. I took out my pen knife – in those days I always carried one – and carefully I trimmed of most of the little bits of fat. I then turned it over the other side to which I gave a little bit of attention. It looked quite good, although there was little wrong in the first place. I sat down for a further fifteen minutes, before returning to the customer. I half ran and hurried up the garden path, panting as though I had been rushing about. I knocked and waited. The mother and daughter greeted me together. I managed to tell them, as I handed over the meat for their inspection, how I had been as quick as I could as I did not want their lunch to be delayed or spoilt.

'What a lovely bit of steak. Why can't Guy send us meat like this in the first place? Thank you, butcher.'

I chuckled to myself as I hurried back up the path. On arrival the shop had been scrubbed and I caught the cricket lorry driven by a cheerful, smiling Alf Turner. His father, George, came as umpire.

John Stenning; A Full Life in Ditchling, Hassocks & Burgess Hill (1998).

Hunting Heroics

Gilbert Sargent, author of these memoirs, was brought up in Catsfield.

The Master of Hounds was a man named Charles Egerton. He was a brother-in-law to the Brasseys, lived at Mountfield, just out of Battle (next to Netherfield) and he was Master of the East Sussex Hunt for nearly twenty seasons, on and off, like. The huntsman was a man named Morgan – George Morgan. He lived at the kennels in Catsfield. D'you know, they once chased an old fox right over the roof of a house in Ninfield? Yeh, fox and hounds right up the cat-slide roof and over into the road on the other side! Absolutely true.

They was very smart, all dressed up in silk hats and red coats, 'hunting pink' they called it. Us kids used to follow them round if we wasn't at school – and sometimes when we was supposed to be at school! We'd open the field gates for them and they'd give us a couple of pennies. It was all very exciting for us.

Have you heard of 'blooding'? What they called 'blooding' was when a boy or girl was in at their first kill and they rubbed blood on their faces from the dead fox. Oh, it was quite a common thing, and they was jolly proud of it an' all, the sons and daughters of the hunt members. They used to cut the old brush off of the dead fox and wipe it on their face and then they'd give 'em the brush as a souvenir, like. They wouldn't wipe it off; they'd leave it on right through dinner. It was a big thing, blooding.

They did the same sort of thing when they was shooting. A lot of the villagers used to go beating, around Ashburnham and Normanhurst, when there was shooting parties, and us kids used to help with carrying bags and food and suchlike. I remember seeing one land having blood rubbed on his cheek after he'd shot his first pheasant. Old Charles Egerton, he crushed the bird's head with his teeth and then wiped all the blood and brains all over the young bloke's face. Then he gave him some of the feathers to wear in his hat, like a badge.

I remember what they called the game larder on the Normanhurst Estate: oh, that were big! It would just about fit in my courtyard outside of where I am now. It was all covered with this here fine gauze with the small holes: you know – even a fly couldn't get through. But they did get on the outside of it and they'd be all over it, and when nobody wasn't looking us kids used to go up and smack the wire or else clap our hands and those flies used to come off in clouds, there was thousands and thousands of them. It was for all the world like a dozen humming-tops going off; then, after a few seconds, they'd all settle back on the outside and we'd give it another smack. They used to have deer carcasses in there: pheasants, rabbits – all sorts. I saw a deer carried in one day with a great big hole in its chest and I heard one of the keepers say as how Lord someone or other, one of the guests, had killed it with a lance. Yeh, a lance! They do some strange things, those upper classes.

Gilbert Sargent; A Sussex Life (1989)

Killed by a Skittles Ball

As Mrs Shepherd, Mistress of the Red Lion public house at Crowborough, was crossing her ninepin alley where some men were at play, she was unhappily struck by the bowl on the temple, which was going at great force, fractured her skull in the most shocking manner. She was soon after trepanned, but to no good effect, as she languished till Saturday, and died in the greatest agony.

Sussex Weekly Advertiser, *June 1796*

A Marathon Walk

The most important sporting event at Horsham . . . that I ever heard of took place in 1823, when a man named Verrall, called the 'Lad', undertook to walk 1000 miles in 20 consecutive days for a wager of £30. Verrall, 43 years of age, married with 11 children, a pig jobber by trade, had fallen upon hard times and decided to try the sporting instincts of the town as a means of improving his fortunes. His walk from the Swann Inn to the Dog and Bacon Inn and back again, a distance of exactly a mile each way, twenty-five times daily, fifty miles a day. He started on Tuesday Nov. 4th 1823 at 4.30am and finished his first day's walk just after 9pm. The next day he started at 4am and finished at 7pm; on Thursday he started at 4.30am and finished 9.30pm. He declared: 'The Lad will not give in until he can go no longer, and of that he is not afraid.' He had had no previous training except the walking from town to town necessitated by his ordinary business. His attempt at such a record met with a great amount of support in the town. The people on the coaches, too, were very interested and also encouraged him. He stuck to his self-imposed task and manfully completed it within the specified time, though he got so sleepy towards the end that he was obliged to have a man to support him and keep him awake. He finished on the night of Sunday Nov. 24th, the old band playing him in at the finish, thus winning his wager and making altogether in winnings and presents £300.

Henry Burstow; Reminiscences of Horsham *(1911)*

Stoolball in Sussex

Not unlike cricket in some respects, stoolball has square 'wickets' on tall posts and is played by both men and women – often in mixed teams.

Often, when I talk about old Sussex pastimes, someone will add the remark that 'stoolball is to Sussex as rugby is to Wales'. The game is certainly played with great enthusiasm in the county at the present time – there are over two hundred teams playing competitively, many more than in the neighbouring counties of Kent, Surrey and Hampshire. But as far back as the 15th century the game was being payed in many other parts of England. In 1450 parish priests were instructed to prevent the game being played in churchyards (unlike cricket, the game does not require an absolutely level ground). . . . Much of our knowledge of the game in earlier days comes from records of complaints made to magistrates concerning the players' preference for playing stoolball rather than attending church.

Many older folk remember stoolball being played in Sussex in their youth. Mrs Richter remembers playing it at Plummers Plain when she was in service in 1909. Mrs Chandler, who was in service at Sheffield Park around the same period, had many happy memories of her team, which was made up of servants and others from the big house. They travelled in a horse and cart, wearing their best clothes, for matches against neighbouring villages and, because these were the only times they ever had an opportunity to leave their own village, they looked upon these outings as tremendous treats.

When World War I put a stop to so many things, stoolball might have been one more casualty, never to have reappeared, had it not been for the enthusiasm of one man, Major W.W. Grantham. At that time he was a familiar figure in the county, wearing his Sussex smock and a beaver hat wherever stoolball was played. He researched the game, made a collection of press cuttings on it and wrote widely about it. His book *Stoolball and how to play it* is, as far as I know, the only book ever written on the sport. The first edition appeared in 1919, and in 1931 he published an enlarged second edition, which includes many references and pictures relating to Sussex.

The spark that started Major Grantham on his one-man crusade on behalf of Sussex stoolball came in July 1917, when the war had been raging for three years, and his eldest son returned from France badly wounded. Looking for a sport that wounded men, such as his own son, might be able to play, he hit upon stoolball as the ideal compromise – not as energetic as tennis or cricket, suitable for any age and either sex, and simple to learn and play.

This wartime revival was largely responsible for the popularity of the game today. There is now a national association, based in Sussex. Fierce competition takes place between teams, both women's and mixed, and as far as this corner of England is concerned the game is in a very healthy state.

Tony Wales; Sussex Customs, Curiosities & Country Lore (1990)

Sporting Epitaphs

Tom Johnson, a leading figure in the then famous Charlton hunt, near Chichester, was a legend in his own lifetime. He died in 1774, and was given a substantial memorial in Singleton church.

> Here JOHNSON lies. What Hunter can deny
> Old honest TOM the Tribute of a Sigh.
> Deaf is the Ear, which caught the opening Sound,
> Dumb is the Tongue, which cheard the Hills around.
> Unpleasing Truth Death hunts us from our Birth
> In view, and Men, like foxes, take to Earth.

Lines by Francis Thompson adorn the gravestone of a keen cricketer, Alban Barchard, at Boxgrove.

> For the field is full of shades
> as I near the shadowy coast
> And a ghostly batsman plays
> to the bowling of a ghost.

One imagines that his nearest and dearest saw little of Richard Pippard (1923–1988), but his humorously succinct epitaph at Cuckfield suggests that he was forgiven.

> Gone fishing

12 · BIRD, BEAST AND FLOWER

Yes, we've already enjoyed plenty of descriptions of towns, villages and landscape in our anthology, but this chapter is given over to nature writing – a rather different kettle of fish, flesh and fowl. These are passages by writers who see, feel and write intensely. A little swooning is grudgingly allowed, but far more important are powers of close observation. Richard Jefferies comes first. He grew up in Wiltshire, but his best work followed his move to Sussex in 1881. Suffering from chronic tuberculosis, he died at the age of just 38 and is buried in Broadwater cemetery. His epitaph reads: 'To the honoured memory of the Prose poet of England's Fields and Woodlands'.

Along the Brighton Line

The smooth express to Brighton has scarcely, as it seems, left the metropolis when the banks of the railway become coloured with wild flowers. Seen for a moment in swiftly passing, they border the line like a continuous garden. Driven from the fields by plough and hoe, cast out from the pleasure-grounds of modern houses, pulled up and hurled over the wall to wither as accursed things, they have taken refuge on the embankment and the cutting.

There they can flourish and ripen their seeds, little harassed even by the scythe and never by grazing cattle. So it happens that, extremes meeting, the wild flower, with its old-world associations, often grows most freely within a few feet of the wheels of the locomotive. Purple heathbells gleam from shrub-like bunches dotted along the slope; purple knapweeds lower down in the grass; blue scabious, yellow hawkweeds where the soil is thinner, and harebells on the very summit; these are but a few upon which the eye lights while gliding by.

Glossy thistledown, heedless whither it goes, comes in at the open window. Between thickets of broom there is a glimpse down into a meadow shadowed by the trees of a wood. It is bordered with the cool green of brake fern, from which a rabbit has come forth to feed, and a pheasant strolls along with a mind, perhaps, to the barley yonder. Or a foxglove lifts its purple spire; or woodbine crowns the bushes. The sickle has gone over, and the poppies which grew so thick a while ago in the corn no longer glow like a scarlet cloak thrown on the ground. But red spots in waste places and by the ways are where they have escaped the steel.

Presently the copses are azure with bluebells, among which the brake is thrusting itself up; others, again, are red with ragged robins, and the fields adjacent fill the eye with the gaudy glare of yellow charlock. The note of the cuckoo sounds above the rushing of the train, and the larks may be seen, if not heard, rising high over the wheat. Some birds, indeed, find the bushes by the railway the quietest place in which to build their nests.

The haze hangs over the wide, dark plain, which, soon after passing Redhill, stretches away on the right. It seems to us in the train to extend from the foot of a great bluff there to the first rampart of the still distant South Downs. In the evening that haze will be changed to a flood of purple light veiling the horizon. Fitful glances at the newspaper or the novel pass the time; but now I can read no longer, for I know, without any marks or tangible evidence, that the hills are drawing near. There is always hope in the hills.

The dust of London fills the eyes and blurs the vision; but it penetrates deeper than that. There is a dust that chokes the spirit, and it is this that makes the streets so long, the stones so stony, the desk so wooden; the very rustiness of the iron railings about the offices sets the teeth on edge, the sooty blackened walls (yet without shadow) thrust back the sympathies which are ever trying to cling to the inanimate things around us. A breeze comes in at the carriage window – a wild puff, disturbing the heated stillness of the summer day. It is easy to tell where that came from – silently the Downs have stolen into sight.

So easy is the outline of the ridge, so broad and flowing are the slopes, that those who have not mounted them cannot grasp the idea of their real height and steepness. The copse upon the summit yonder looks but a short stroll distant; how much you would be deceived did you attempt to walk thither! The ascent here in front seems nothing, but you must rest before you have reached a third of the way up. Ditchling Beacon there, on the left, is the very highest above the sea of the whole mighty range, but so great is the mass of the hill that the glance does not realise it.

Hope dwells there, somewhere, mayhap, in the breeze, in the sward, or the pale cups of the harebells. Now, having gazed at these, we can lean back on the cushions and wait patiently for the sea. There is nothing else, except the noble sycamores on the left hand just before the train draws into the station.

Richard Jefferies 'To Brighton' from Nature Near London (1905)

Discovering Kingley Vale

Richard Williamson, son of the Tarka the Otter author, came to Sussex from East Anglia to manage the Kingley Vale nature reserve with its ancient yew forest and (as he quickly discovered) much else besides. Here he recalls the very first exploration of his new territory.

I wandered on, into the valley and its woodlands encircling the path. At first the valley slopes on either side rose gently and were wide apart; ahead I could see that they narrowed and ended abruptly in a very steep hill. These slopes were covered with a dense yew forest, crown upon crown touching and leaving no opening, a canopy of dark green. Thus they formed an amphitheatre, and in the pit of this I felt small – not insignificant, but rather, out of place. The human shape intruded within this natural landscape, as it would not in any man-made countryside. Deeper into the wood I went, and came upon some ancient trees whose boughs drooped around them and touched the ground. These yews, when I had penetrated one of the few cleft entrances under their hanging crowns, were of weird shapes. The trunks were ruddy brown, smooth, but twisted and bulging with a dozen secret recesses where wrens could nest and squirrels hide themselves. I could only guess the girth, but thought that it might be well over twenty feet. One monster had grown such a long bough that this had broken near the trunk and now hung down with a splintered gape like a crocodile's mouth.

These were no carefully kept and propped-up churchyard yews with concreted cavities – they were wild and hoary with age, they saw the passing of deer and fox and had weathered a thousand winters. From the crowns, drooping bines of clematis hung down to the ground like liana stems, thick as ships' ropes, forming an enclosed, dry place like the inside of a church. On this humid autumn day it was cool. It would be a wonderful place in the height of summer. The ground was bare – no grass, no plants of any kind. Perhaps this was due to the lack of light? Around the roots I could see, when my eyes were used to the gloom, those red waxy blobs that had been growing on the twigs. I had no idea what kind of fruit the yew tree bore, and had imagined a small fir cone. But here it was, a red, soft cup, fleshy and smooth, not much larger than a pea. The berries hung on the twigs above, like Chinese lanterns; they looked good to eat.

Standing still and looking around I noticed a mistle thrush feasting on the waxy berries, and then another and another, everywhere I looked. They were not all mistle thrushes either – some were the small cousins, song thrushes. They slipped in and out of sight as they moved from twig to twig. The whole forest was moving with thrushes, and I became aware of a subdued, almost whispering sound, which was the myriads of song thrushes quietly singing to themselves. This was the subsong that I had heard individual birds singing in the autumn hedges at home. I had never heard a choir of birds performing. The soft whistles merged from all sides of the enclosed valley as though I were, again, within a vast building, but one with a roof open to the sky. For there, above all the song, the birds, the wild flowers and clusters of dark trees, was the autumn sky going from blue to a smoky gold – early afternoon yet, and a more dusky colour than I was used to in the clean open skies of the east. Already part of the valley was in shade, its western side where a grove of ash trees grew among the yew forest, stretching up for five hundred feet to the hill.

Richard Williamson; The Great Yew Forest (1978)

Mondays on Ashdown Forest

Barbara Willard found Monday the most magical day on Ashdown Forest because all the visitors had departed, leaving it to the grateful residents.

In the quiet of Monday morning the Forest is like some vast room whose windows have been flung wide. If there is a problem it is merely that one of choice – which outlook, which best loved tree-line or twist of running water? From the high ground the views are of surrounding hills, the South Downs, the Surrey hills – or there is that one spot where you may rotate to identify four counties. I would always favour the southern aspect, probably because I was there before I was here. It is best on a day with big clouds, none darker than a mild grey, the rest blinding white and gently bowling across the sun. Against such a background the downs are sharp and clear though without that sharpness that brings them close and foretells rain. Heads can be counted from Wilmington to Firle, by Blackcap, by Ditchling Beacon to Truleigh, Chanctonbury, Cissbury. On certain rare October evenings when the light is changing it is possible to see still further west – though I may have been indulging myself once when I imagined Duncton.

That is a rare and exalting light, while on a chosen Monday morning in summer there is a workaday light. The wind at that season is probably a little south of south-west, soft on the cheek, comfortable. It carries, or seems to carry, a reminder of the sea. That may be the scent of bracken, which has a slightly briny tang to it. At this season it spreads such a dense green sea of its own that the smaller paths, those that are little more than deer runs, are pretty well swallowed. Any walker who knows them can just about push through waist high, more than waist high. The thought of adders, however, brings caution to the native. Leave them alone and they slip smoothly on their way; but in a brackeny situation it is too easy to step on the creatures, for the dog to step on them, and they will not accept rough treatment without retaliation.

Summer, even on the acclaimed Monday morning, is by no means the best season for the Forest. Autumn cannot fail to offer more than any other time. Spring is just spring, exuberant, delicate and a bit silly, following the inevitable pattern, an infinity of subtly differing greens, bluebell, wood anemone – few primroses here. When the bracken first breaks through it has some charm, acres of mock asparagus far removed from that later sea, so heavy and unvaried, so downright boring. The initial hint of better things comes after the orchids, the first-footer among the heathers, delicately pink and immensely welcome. There is a fractional pause, then, almost a change of light. The purple heathers take up the theme, with *erica tetralix*, the cross-leaved heath, surely the winner for its exhuberant colour and dark shape leaf. The less well-coloured ling then takes over, swamping all. Sheets of the stuff are spread like tented cloth. As if infected by the basic dye, the bracken begins to turn. When this happens it is difficult to understand why one has ever supposed it a mere invader. It complements all, not least the marsh gentian which is the Forest's pride. Impossible, when bracken is at the peak of its colour, to have too much of it – or so many of us claim. It is not only autumn, either, that gives it so long a splendour – wet winter restores colour to the battered rows and they glow again.

Barbara Willard; The Forest (1989)

Memoirs of a Herb Collector

Walter Murray's book tells a familiar story, of a sophisticated townie discovering rural Sussex, in this case taking over a delapidated cottage near Horam. The twist to the tale was that he had decided to earn a living by collecting, drying and selling herbs. Needless to say, he didn't make a fortune, but he survived a full season after a fashion. Later he was to found an independent coeducational school in Horam and become an acclaimed nature photographer.

I dawdled over the gathering of sweet-chestnut leaves. Not only was it my last harvest, but the woods were so exquisitely lovely and the autumnal atmosphere so golden and yellow that linger I must. I would pick a bagful, almost as light as a feather-filled pillow, and on some sun-dappled knoll recline with my back against it and fall into timeless contempaltion. I saw without looking. I heard without listening. I perceived without reasoning. I became a part of the woods. The long husk of the midday breeze whispered about me and in it I heard the response of ten thousand choirs of tiny voices. It was the slow movement, the *andante*, of a great choral symphony in which all the muted strings quivered in tremulous spiccato, loud, apassionato, wave on wave, advancing, receding, flooding in, and then rippling and all a-shimmer, like the trembling surface of a lake alive with evening light.

With the first sharp November frosts the leaves fell. They showered down in inconceivable multitudes. The slightest breath of air seemed as though it must denude the trees to the very last twig. But there were always more, and the next chilly draw of frosty air brought another twinkling shower of greens and yellows, gold and bronze, brown and crimson. I could never restrain the impulse to dart among the shower and catch a falling leaf.

Walter Murray; Copsford (1948)

Paradise at Perch Hill

The writer Adam Nicolson moved to a farm in the Sussex countryside with his wife and young family – and this is their story. Perch Hill is in Kipling country, up in the north east of the county.

By mid-morning the work was done, I'd had breakfast and I'd got the day free. I don't understand how sunshine works, but everything that morning looked as if it had acquired another dimension. Far to the east, for 12 miles or so to the hills above Rye, it was so clear that I felt I could see the individual trees. Westwards I could surely make out the slats in the sails of the Punnett's Town mill, which is a good hour and a half's walk from here. Was all this simply the sharpness and clarity of rain-washed air? Whatever it was, the whole place looked like a glass of white wine tastes.

I went down to the Slip Field. It is the one field on the farm that we all love best here, and that day it was wearing its midsummer clothes. It is a south-facing bank of about two and a half acres surrounded on all sides by wood: the oak and hazel of the middle shaw to the right, the long frondy arms of the ashes in the Ashwood Shaw to the left and, in front of me, at the foot of the hillside, the two acres of garlic flowering then in the hazelwood shade of Coombe Wood, a stinking, lush and frothy garden which squeaked as you walked through it at that time of year with the big, rubberised, smelly leaves rubbing up against your shins.

It was the field itself which was the zone of heaven that day. Its slippy soil meant that it had never been reseeded with commercial grass mixture and so here, between the garlic and the bluebell woods, hidden from the world but open to the sun, was our field of flowers. There were sheets and sheets of the yellow vetch with blood-red tips called eggs and bacon. Here the common blue butterflies flitted in pairs, their blue backs just greying to silver along the outer margins of the wing. Curiously, those precise colours, and their relationship, a silvery lining to an eye-blue wing, was exactly repeated in the speedwells that grew in mats among the yellow vetches. Beyond these beds of eggs and bacon, with a scatter of blue among and above them, where the dog and I were both warmly lying, the buttercups and daisies, with pink fringes to their flowers, spread out to the margins of the woods where the pyramidal bugles clustered a darker blue against the one or two bluebells that had leaked out into the field. The dyer's greenweed was not yet in flower and only some tiny forget-me-nots and the taller spiky speedwells added to the picture. A holly tree on the edge of the wood had turned pale with its clusters of white flowers.

A slight wind started the field nodding and other butterflies cruised and flickered in. A pale tortoiseshell hung for a minute on the vetches, followed by a bumblebee which pushed its entire body inside the blooms. A big cabbage white flirted with the nettles and the balsam at the top of the field and then two brown moths, each the size of a fingernail, came dancing in a woven spiral across the hillside, as close in with each other, as bound to and as mobile with each other as the different parts of a guttering flame. The whole world was needled with birdsong, a clustered shrieking sharpness, interrupted only by the jay's coarse squawking, the sudden dropping-off *dwaark* of pheasants and, behind it all, the continuous, laid-back strumming of the woodland bassists, the pigeons in their five-part, broken-backed rhythm, two rising, a pause, two falling, doo-doo, doo, doo-doo, the only soundtrack you need for an English summer.

Adam Nicolson, Perch Hill *(1999)*

13 · LAST LINES

*For many people nothing but rhymed verse is suitable for marking
great occasions, and here are some notable examples on gravestones.
Inevitably these efforts often fall far short of poetry, but we begin with
an exception. The eccentric John Olliver was an educated miller who
prepared for death well in advance, keeping his coffin under the bed
for many years before his death in 1793. His tomb can be seen, not in
a churchyard but up on the Downs at Highdown, above Worthing.
The words are his own.*

> Death, why so fast? Pray stop your hand
> And let my glass run out its sand:
> As neither Death nor Time will stay,
> Let us improve the present day.
> Why start you at that skeleton?
> 'Tis your own picture which you shun.
> Alive it did resemble thee
> And thou when dead like that shall be:
> But tho' Death must have his will,
> Yet old Time prolongs the date,
> Till the measure we shall fill
> That's allotted us by Fate.

When that's done, then TIME and DEATH
Both agree to take our breath!

Altogether more jovial is the epitaph to Michael Turner, clerk and sexton at Warnham for 50 years until his death in 1885.

His duty done, beneath this stone
   Old Michael liest at rest.
His rustic rig, his song, his jib
   Were ever of the best.

With nodding head the choir he led
   That none should start too soon.
The second, too, he sang full true,
   His viol played the tune.

And when at last his age had passed
   One hundred less eleven
With faithful cling to fiddle string
   He sang himself to heaven.

Another church 'character' was John Alcorn. He died in 1868 at the age of 81, having been parish clerk at Worth for many years.

The lich-gate's shadow o'er his pall at last
Bids kind adieu as poor old John goes past:
Unseen the path, the trees, the old oak door;
No more his footfalls touch the tomb-paved floor:
His silvery head is hid, his service done,
Of all those sabbaths absent only one.
And now amid the graves he delved around
He rests and sleeps beneath the hallowed ground.

Although disease took many away in centuries past, the cause of death isn't often alluded to. Sarah White's gravestone can be seen in the tower Cocking church, and it's specific. She died in 1772 at the age of 25. 'Crave' here means 'fear'.

Weep not for me my parents dear
Since God was pleased to lay me here.
It was the smallpox I did crave
Which now has brought me to my grave.

There's something rather chilling about the bald verse on the tomb
of young John Parson, who died at West Tarring in 1683. That
youth, virginity and learning have come to nothing.

> Youth was his age,
> Virginity his state,
> Learning his love
> Consumption his fate.

Mary Atkinson was a Chichester winkle seller who died in 1786. Her
gravestone is, alas, no longer to be found, but such is the wit of
epitaph writers that we have no reason to doubt that it existed . . .

> Periwinkle! Periwinkle!
> Was ever her cry.
> She laboured to live,
> Poor and honest to die.
> At the last day again
> Her old eyes will twinkle,
> For no more will they say
> Periwink, Periwinkle!

But the very last word must belong to Alice Wooldridge, who died
at Poling on May 27, 1740. It has a touch of the music hall about it,
and has the virtue of being unanswerable.

> The World is a round thing,
> And full of crooked streets.
> Death is a market-place
> Where all men meets.
> If Life was a thing
> That money could buy,
> The Rich would live
> And the Poor would die.

ACKNOWLEDGEMENTS

I am grateful to authors and publishers for permission to reproduce material which is still in copyright. Where possible I have used extracts entire, but on occasions I have either omitted paragraphs or words within paragraphs – in the latter case indicating the elision with a row of dots (although, to confuse the issue, some authors are in the habit of including their own dots without intending to send the same signal). There has been a little tidying of punctuation, particularly in the earliest extracts, but I trust that the only insult I can be judged to have inflicted lies in not having had space to do greater justice to the original texts.

My thanks to: Wordsworth Editions for Rudyard Kipling's *Rewards & Fairies, They* and *Sussex*; *The Four Men* reprinted by permission of PFD on behalf of The Estate of Hilaire Belloc © 1923, Hilaire Belloc; Bob Copper for *Early to Rise* and *A Song for Every Season*; Doreen Darby for Ben Darby's *View of Sussex* and *The South Downs*; Susan Row for Frank Dean's *Strike while the iron's hot* and Harold Cannings' *Follow the plough*; The Society of the Friends of Ashdown Forest and Garth Christian for *Ashdown Forest*; Countryside Books on behalf of Ensign Publications for Tony Wales' *Sussex Customs, Curiosities & Country Lore*; the extract from Dirk Bogarde's *A Postillion Struck by Lightning*, published by Chatto & Windus and reprinted by permission of The Random House Group Ltd; from *Deceived with Kindness* by Angelica Garnett, published by Chatto & Windus and reprinted by permission of The Random House Group Ltd; The Barclay Wills Estate and Methuen (*Shepherds of Sussex*); Robert Hale for Michael Baker's *Sussex Scenes*; S.B. Publications for Jim Etherington's *Lewes Bonfire Night*, Andy Thomas's *Streets of Fire*, W.H. Johnson's *Seaside Entertainment* and David Harries' *Maritime Sussex*; A & C Black for George Aitchison's *Sussex* and W. Harding Thompson & Geoffrey Clark's *The Sussex Landscape*; for the extract reproduced by kind permission from *The South Downs* by Peter Brandon, published in 1998 by Phillimore & Co Ltd, Shopwyke Manor Barn, Chichester, West Sussex PO20 2BG;

for the extract from *Sussex: People, Places, Things* by Bernard Price, published in 1975 by Phillimore & Co Ltd, Shopwyke Manor Barn, Chichester, West Sussex PO20 2BG; Sheil Land Associates Ltd for Desmond Seward's *Sussex*, first published by Pimlico, an imprint of Random House, 1995; Tempus Publishing for Jill Eddison's *Romney Marsh*; The Dovecote Press for John E. Vigar's *The Lost Villages of Sussex*; QueenSpark Books for Bert Healey's *Hard Times & Easy Terms* and James Nye's *A Small account of my travels through the wilderness;* David Atkins and the Dovecote Press for *The Cuckoo in June;* the Royal Pavilion, Libraries & Museums, Brighton & Hove for Richard Marks' *Sussex Churches & Chapels*; Yale University Press for Ian Nairn's *The Buildings of England: Sussex*; Newsbooks for Steve Peak's *Fishermen of Hastings*; Paul Foster and Bishop Otter College, Chichester for *A Jewel in Stone*; Pallas Athene for Pieter Boogaart's *A272 An Ode to a Road*; Penguin Books for Eve Garnett's *The Family from One End Street* published by Puffin Modern Classics, 1942, copyright © Eve Garnett, 1942; David Higham Associates and Random House for Graham Greene's *Brighton Rock*; Macdonald for John Cowper Powys' *Autobiography*; E.F. Benson's *Lucia's Progress* reproduced by permission of A.P. Watt Ltd on behalf of The Executors of the Estate of K.S.P. McDowall; Penguin Books for Stella Gibbons' *Cold Comfort Farm*; Richard Masefield for *Chalkhill Blue*; The Sussex Archaeological Society for *A Lewes Diary 1916–1944*; Robert Edwards for *Attitude to Sussex*; Country Books for John Stenning's *A Full Life in Ditchling, Hassocks & Burgess Hill*; Chapel Press for Gilbert Sargent's *A Sussex Life*; Macmillan Publishers for Richard Williamson's *The Great Yew Forest*; HarperCollins and Allen & Unwin for Walter Murray's *Copsford*; Sweethaws Press for Barbara Willard's *The Forest*; Constable & Robinson and Adam Nicolson for *Perch Hill*; for the extract from *The Diaries of Virginia Woolf, Vol 1, 1915-1919*, published by the Hogarth Press, reprinted by permission of the executors of the Estate of Virginia Woolf and The Random House Group Ltd; an extract from *Joanna Godden* by Sheila Kaye Smith, reprinted by permission of PFD on behalf of The Estate of Sheila Kaye Smith, © 1921, Sheila Kaye Smith.

The publishers have endeavoured to contact all holders of copyright, but will be pleased to correct any omissions or errors in future editions.